seventeen
ULTIMATE GUIDE TO
GUYS

What He *Really* Thinks About
Flirting, Dating, Relationships, and YOU!

ANN SHOKET
& THE EDITORS OF *seventeen*

EDITED
by
BETHANY HEITMAN

RUNNING PRESS
PHILADELPHIA · LONDON

HI FROM
ann!

If you could have any super power what would you choose? The ability to fly? Sure, the view would be great. Super strength? That might come in handy during sports practice. But what about the **power to know what guys are thinking** during a flirty text convo, date, or makeout session? Yes, please!

This book is better than having a super power. Dozens of guys told *Seventeen* exactly what they think when it comes to **flirting, dating, hooking up, and falling in love.** Some of the confessions will make you melt, some may surprise you, but all of them will help you **understand guys** on a deeper level than you ever have before!

Armed with that juicy intel, you're setting yourself up for **total dating confidence!** No more second guessing yourself: You'll know the right flirting moves to make, the **secret weapon** that makes him worship you, and the sneaky way to define the relationship so you can avoid that awkward convo!

At *Seventeen,* it's our mission to make sure your life—especially your love life—is **totally amazing** in every way. Get ready to be your own dating superhero!

XOXO
-A.

FLIRT
like an
all-star

MAKE THE RIGHT
first impression!

He'll form his initial thoughts about you three seconds into your very first convo—and you want them to be good! How exactly do you pull that off? This section is going to make you the girl that he just can't . . . stop . . . thinking about . . . (In the best way!) Let's get started!

SNEAKY WAYS
to score flirting *confidence!*

Practice these moves now—and then every convo you have with a super-hot guy will feel like NBD!

1
flirt with the waiter.

Try your moves on a guy who doesn't really matter to you so that you have a non-scary way to figure out what works: what makes a guy laugh, what makes him roll his eyes, etc. A cute waiter is the perfect test-run because it's his job to pay attention to you!

2
warm up on text.

It's easier to say something bold to your crush over text, and when you get in the habit of throwing out those lines (and realize that most of the time they totally work!), you'll eventually get the guts to try it in person. Just hit *send* already!

3
learn to speak "guy."

When you're hanging out with your guy friends, pay attention to what they talk about and what cracks them up. Being totally comfortable in guy-world helps you hold your own around a cutie you like, and may even give you a few jokes to steal.

4
play wing girl.

When you're acting as the sidekick for a flirty friend, you get to be part of the action without any pressure. Seeing how she talks to guys will rub off on you—soon you'll be ready to jump right in.

signs he wants you to *make a move*

Breaking news: Your crush is probably just as nervous as you are! Here's how to tell if he's dying for *you* to take action.

HE DOES THE "LOOK BACK."

When he passes you in the hall and then looks back at you again, it means he wants to say something (but he's too intimidated to stop and talk).

HE UNCROSSES HIS ARMS.

More than half of personal communication is done through body language. When a guy positions himself with his hands in his pockets and his elbows away from his body, he is sending the signal that he is open to you—and that he wants you to feel comfortable standing closer to him!

HE TILTS HIS HEAD.

This subtle move is a signal that he wants to understand you and is really interested in what you're saying. Watch his pupils—if they dilate while he's talking to you, he's actually feeling an attraction toward you!

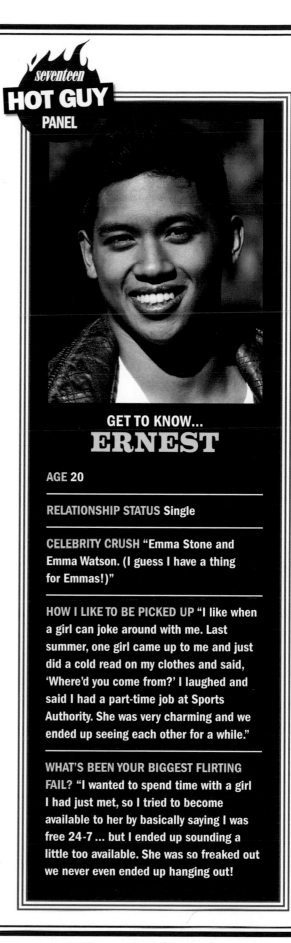

seventeen
HOT GUY PANEL

GET TO KNOW...
ERNEST

AGE 20

RELATIONSHIP STATUS Single

CELEBRITY CRUSH "Emma Stone and Emma Watson. (I guess I have a thing for Emmas!)"

HOW I LIKE TO BE PICKED UP "I like when a girl can joke around with me. Last summer, one girl came up to me and just did a cold read on my clothes and said, 'Where'd you come from?' I laughed and said I had a part-time job at Sports Authority. She was very charming and we ended up seeing each other for a while."

WHAT'S BEEN YOUR BIGGEST FLIRTING FAIL? "I wanted to spend time with a girl I had just met, so I tried to become available to her by basically saying I was free 24-7 ... but I ended up sounding a little too available. She was so freaked out we never even ended up hanging out!

have the

No more excuses ... no more

"I have nothing to say."

"I'm not the prettiest girl in the room."

"If he wanted to talk to me, he'd come talk to me."

"I'll die of embarrassment if he rejects me."

perfect first convo!

stressing out! These super-easy tricks will help you two totally hit it off!

GET OVER IT!

GET THE BALL ROLLING: You don't have to be loaded with fascinating facts to talk to dudes—you just have to listen to what they're saying and ask questions in a cool, casual way. When you **seem genuinely interested,** it makes people want to keep talking. (So the pressure is off you.)

BE THE COOLEST: Being easy to talk to is about knowing how to steer the conversation in interesting directions—like by **chuckling at his jokes, cracking your own, or playfully arguing about movies**—and not at all about what you look like. It's about what will make every guy feel comfortable around you!

MAKE THE FIRST MOVE: You have *no* idea what's going through his head. He might be painfully shy, worried you'll reject him, or he could be thinking the same thing about you! Don't let your assumptions hold you back from giving it a shot. **Be the more confident person** and start the conversation first.

GET GUTSY: The potential for a great connection totally outweighs the chance that he's not interested. Worst-case scenario: He's not. Then just escape gracefully by saying to him, "Okay, I'm gonna take a lap. Nice talking to ya!" **At least then you'll never wonder,** What if I'd talked to him?

SNEAKY TIP

BE PREPARED: Start the conversation with a few stock questions. ("What have you been up to?" or "Have you ever seen this group live?") Then **look for a way to drop in a few of your stories,** so he can ask you Qs!

ACT FAST: When you debate for half of the party if you should talk to him, your anxiety just builds. So **channel your cool-girl vibe** and vow to approach him within the first three seconds you see him!

FEEL OUT HIS INTEREST: Ask a casual question to put his nerves at ease. ("Do you think it's okay if I parked in the driveway?") If he gives you his full attention, great. If not, whatever—it was hardly a confession of love!

HOT GUY PANEL

BE APPROACHABLE
"Smile! No matter what we talk about, that's what I'll remember."
–Connor

ENLIST A FRIEND: Tag along while she approaches your crush's friend, so all four of you can talk. That way **you'll get a chance to hit it off**—but won't have to zero in on him right away (no chance for rejection!).

talk to *any* guy!

Keep these dude-approved ways to say
hi to any guy in your back pocket, just in case!

SNEAK HIM YOUR NUMBER.

66 At a big party, a girl I had been pursuing came up to me and grabbed my phone. She put her number in it before handing it back to me and then walked away. Not only was it creative, but it was also a very confident move that I found immediately attractive—I texted her back right away. 99

–ANDREW, 19

USE A SLICK LINE.

66 I was in the kitchen at a party when this girl asked if I wanted a drink—she said she'd grabbed an extra for her friend but couldn't find her. I took it, and we ended up talking for the rest of the night. Later she confessed that she made it up as an excuse to talk to me. It worked! 99

–RYAN, 18

GO FOR A WALK.

66 I was at a super-crowded party, and I really hit it off with the girl I was talking to. At the end of the night, she said, 'Do you want to go for a walk?' I was pumped! It was a very casual way to initiate some one-on-one time, which gave me the perfect excuse to get her number. 99

–NICHOLAS, 19

BUY AHEAD.

66 I was paying for coffee at Starbucks when a girl interrupted me and said it was on her. I turned around, and she said, 'I love your smile and just couldn't pass up the chance to talk to you.' It was definitely a ballsy move!' 99

–CHAD, 19

BE BOLD

66 If we meet at a party, put your hand on my arm and tell me your name. That kind of confidence is hot! 99

–CHRIS

TAKE THE SEAT NEXT TO HIM.

66 When a cute girl sits next to me in class, I notice. Once a girl caught me checking her out and called me on it. It was sassy—I loved it! 99

–DYLAN, 18

THE
flirting
moves
HE'LL ♥

Whether you've known your crush since kindergarten or you just met him at a cool college party, it's not just about catching his attention . . . it's about maintaining it! It's fun to come up with cute text ideas, but how will you know if your moves work? Here, dudes explain the difference between what's hot . . . and the oh-so-major fails. Follow their advice, and you'll leave your guy wanting more every time you talk!

cute *vs.* creepy

Know how to leave your guy dying to see
you again—not secretly thinking you're a nut job!

DROPPING BY...

CUTE **Surprising him in public.** "I love when a girl unexpectedly shows up at one of my sports games to cheer me on. But the best is when she hangs around for a few extra minutes— just to say hi—when I'm on my way back to the locker room with the team. Having a fan is very rock star."
  –JOHN, 18

CREEPY! **Surprising him at home.** "I got back to my dorm after a full day of classes, and this girl in my psych class was at my desk waiting for me. Maybe she thought it was 'spontaneous,' but I was freaked out. Waiting around for someone is total stalker behavior!"
  –TRAVIS, 18

HANGING OUT...

CUTE **Stealing the spotlight.** "I went to dinner with a big group of friends, and while we waited for our table, one girl launched into this hilarious story that kept us all entertained. It made her seem really cool—I found myself wondering what it would be like to date her."
  –CARTER, 18

CREEPY! **Hogging the spotlight.** "I met this cute girl at a party, and our conversation turned to special talents. She told me she's awesome at imitating animal noises—then let out this extremely loud 'call of the wild.' Everyone stared at her, and I was horrified."
  –NEILL, 18

KEEPING IN TOUCH...

CUTE **Leaving a sweet VM.** "One time I was on vacation overseas, and I didn't have phone service. When I came back and turned on my cell, I had a few charming voicemails from this girl saying how much she missed me. It was so much more personal to hear her voice—not just a text."
  –CALEB, 19

CREEPY! **Leaving a million messages.** "This girl I was flirting with over Facebook started posting on my wall a lot. When I stopped responding, she'd post multiple messages in a row. If a guy ignores more than two messages, take a hint. It felt like she was trying to scare off other girls!"
  –LORENZO, 20

DRESSING UP...

CUTE **Wearing what makes you happy.** "I love girls who can rock jeans and high-top sneakers. When you can dress down for a party and still look cute, you seem confident and easy-going— not like you're trying to impress. Every guy is drawn to the girl who looks totally comfortable in her own skin."
  –NICK, 20

CREEPY! **Changing to make him happy.** "Once at a party, this girl asked what kind of clothes I like on a girl. I was caught off guard, but I said, 'Um, really short shorts?' Then she went upstairs and came back in these tiny little shorts! Who does that?!?"
  –BRANDEN, 17

WORST MOVES EVER!

Caution: Trying to get his attention like this will result in a big-time traumarama!

FAIL! *The silent treatment.*
"I was hanging out with a bunch of friends, including a girl who I could tell was trying to flirt with me. She kept coming up to me and touching my back and stomach, but she wasn't saying anything. She would just touch me for a couple seconds and then do it again five minutes later. It was obvious that she was flirting with me, but it just made me super annoyed."

–Josh, 20

Creeping his sched. "I started to notice that the girl I was seeing just 'happened' to be in the hallway whenever I was. She must have memorized my class schedule! Talk about creepy."

–Willie, 20

FAIL! *Breaking and entering.* "A girl I wasn't really into showed up at my house in the middle of the night unannounced and tried to break into my room and surprise me. It didn't come off as flirty. It came off as crazy."

–Alden, 19

Playing dumb. "One time a girl asked me to help her with her homework because she 'didn't get it.' She was playing with her hair and giggling, and it seemed like it was just an excuse to flirt. I don't think most guys are into the whole playing helpless thing."

–Tim, 20

FAIL! *Stealing his phone.*
"This girl kept talking to me and it was obvious that she was trying to get my attention. At the end of the night she 'playfully' took my phone when I was texting someone and she wouldn't give it back, which was really annoying. It backfired because she was trying way too hard to get me."

–Mattan, 19

Acting jealous. "The jealousy thing is the worst! One time, a girl I was into started talking about other guys pursuing her. It made me feel like there was too much competition to even try."

–Myles, 20

make him remember you!

The no-fail way to make a good *lasting* impression? Make him laugh! These guys have a few ideas …

MEMORIZE AN LOL-WORTHY QUOTE

"Guys all have the same interests and find the same things funny. So if a girl quotes anything from *Family Guy* or a Will Ferrell movie, she's hilarious!"
–JOSEPH, 22

LOOSEN UP!

"Guys love when you can genuinely poke fun at the ketchup on your shirt or mismatched socks. It's those little in-the-moment comments that really crack us up!"
–ERNEST

SELL IT

"This girl I know is so confident when telling jokes. Her voice gets louder, and she'll tell everyone to listen. There has never been a time when no one laughed!"

–JJ, 21

BE EXTREME

"At a party if a guy asks, 'How do you know everyone here?' answer with something totally out there, like 'Oh, we all climbed Mount Everest together.'"

–BRIAN, 22

DO VOICES

"It's cute when a girl does impersonations. Like, if she tries to make a tough-guy voice, it's hilarious. She's trying so hard to get you to laugh—it's endearing."

–MARC, 21

PULL A PRANK

"At lunch I threw sugar at a girl, then later my notebooks went missing. I got them back filled with sugar and a note that said, 'Sweet revenge!'"

–JOHN, 23

BTW: THREE THINGS HE'LL NEVER REMEMBER...

1

LABELS

He isn't looking at the distinctive pockets of designer jeans; his eyes are only on your cute butt! Save your splurge clothes for the people who notice—your girlfriends.

2

YOUR BODY HANG-UPS

Are you obsessed with the numbers on your scale? Well, your guy couldn't care less about how much you weigh. If he likes the way you look, he likes the way you look. Seriously!

3

YOUR NEW HAIRCUT

He sees the whole you, not every wisp of your bangs or layers. Don't worry if he doesn't comment. He likes your entire style, so he's not stuck on the details.

seventeen
HOT GUY PANEL

GET TO KNOW...
CONNOR

AGE 17

RELATIONSHIP STATUS Single

CELEBRITY CRUSH Miley Cyrus

HOW I LIKE TO BE PICKED UP "I like to be picked up when I don't know I'm getting picked up! For example, when I notice that a girl is actually listening to me, or just touching me or smiling."

MY BIGGEST FLIRTING FAIL "I was at a party and finally got the nerve to go talk to this girl. Once I got up to her, I could see all my friends watching. I said 'Hey, what's up?' and right afterward, her boyfriend came over and started making out with her right in front of me! Then he just looked at me and said, 'Mine.' I ended up walking back to my friends, all of them bagging on me."

SNEAKY WAYS
to get *past* "just friends"!

So, you're already close with your crush?
Here's how to drop the hint that you want to be *more*.

sneak into his routine!

"Every day, my girl friend would stop by my lunch table to talk. I got used to seeing her regularly and started looking forward to her dropping by. One day it hit me that I wanted to spend even more time with her."

–Michael, 19

send a foolproof message.

"After a big party, one of my girl friends texted me to say that she always got a little jealous when she saw me with other girls. Instantly I realized I felt the same way when I saw her with other guys. Her bold text took our relationship to the next level."

–Erik, 21

show a little tenderness.

"One day my best girl friend and I were watching a movie and pigging out. Suddenly she leaned over, laughed that I had my food on my face, and brushed it off with her napkin. It was a small gesture, but in that instant, I saw her as more than a friend—she was someone who really cared about me."

–Jarett, 16

break off from the pack.

"My friends and I would always hang out in a big group, but when one of the girls in our crew invited me to a school event, just us, it was like a lightbulb in my brain that she liked me as more than a friend. We started dating soon after that."

–Zack, 21

tell him already!

"I'd been flirting with one of my girl friends for months, but I was too nervous to take it beyond that—until she flat out asked me, 'Should we try to make a relationship work?' I was so happy—and said yes right away!"

–Thomas, 19

#17GuyQ

Q: Would you want your best girl friend to tell you if she has feelings for you?

A: "Of course! If we're friends, that means we already know a lot about each other and like doing the same things—and that makes for the perfect romantic relationship. Your guy might think he'll ruin your friendship if he makes the first move, so don't be afraid—tell him how you feel!"
–ZACH, 17

CAN YOU ESCAPE THE FRIEND ZONE?

If three or more of these statements apply, chances are *preeetty* good that he wants to take things to the next level!

☐ You text or Facebook chat at least two times a day.

☐ He asks a lot of questions about you hanging out with other guys.

☐ You're the first one he calls when he's upset about something.

☐ He sometimes talks about other girls—but never goes after them.

☐ He makes up a funny nickname for you that no one else uses.

REALLY
wow
HIM!

Sometimes, it doesn't take any thinking at all to impress your crush. There are tons of hot things you do on a daily basis—even just raising your hand and saying something smart in class!—that guys love. Here, they share all the secret girl-behaviors that do it for them. Take note!

what *really* turns him on!

Without further ado… all the many things that make him want you bad.

positivity!

"I love a girl who has an optimistic personality! There are lots of good-looking girls, but she needs to be fun!"

–Austin, 19

honesty!

"Guys can tell when you're pretending you like something just because they do. I'm more impressed when a girl can share her own opinions!"

–Dan

seventeen **HOT GUY** PANEL

intelligence!

"I'm secretly really into nerdy girls. She will always have something interesting to talk about, she will really appeal to my parents, and if I should need it, she can give me extra help with my homework, too."

–Justin, 20

attitude!

"I'm very sarcastic, and it's such a big turn-on when a girl can dish it back to me!

–Andrew, 22

"There are a few things that are important to me in a girl: honesty, loyalty, the ability to make fun of herself, and the ability to laugh a lot."
–Taylor Lautner

the LITTLE things...

whispering in his ear.

"Sometimes at a party you have to yell over loud music, but if instead you lean in and whisper in my ear ... that's so hot."

–Ryan, 21

indulging in your guy side.

"I went to a hockey game with my girlfriend and when the players got into a fight, she liked it as much as I did! I love to watch sports, so to share that with a girl is a big turn-on."

–Jacob, 20

returning his gaze.

"Say you're in study hall, doing your work, and you suddenly glance at me from across the room, then turn away when our eyes meet—that is so cute. It sparks my imagination and makes me wonder what you're all about."

–Mike, 19

taking charge!

"I love when girls initiate plans instead of being like, 'Whatever you want to do!' Then I know she'll have fun—and it takes the pressure off me."

–Jack, 20

a flirty signal!

"I'm very flirtatious, and I like a girl who is too. Quickly tossing your hair back as we're talking or giving a cute wink as you walk away is great."

–Giuseppe

touching him casually.

"When you 'accidentally' brush your leg against mine when we're sitting next to each other, it's subtle—but effective."

–Martin, 17

bringing the fun!

"My girlfriend is always up for doing small errands with me—from getting my car serviced to picking birthday gifts for my family. It doesn't feel like a chore with her."

–Naz, 19

"[I'm drawn to] someone who's funny. I like to laugh. But I need someone smart. I don't want to talk to someone who's dumb. I want to have an actual conversation with a girl, and I don't want to feel like I'm interviewing her. I don't want to have to ask her what her favorite color is."

–Justin Bieber

girls guys *love*

You have celeb crushes and so does he! Find out who dudes dig, then steal their moves!

bold energy

"**Zendaya** radiates confidence and has that down-to-earth vibe that always makes me want to see what she does next. She's not afraid to push the boundaries."
–ANDREW, 19

a sexy smile

"**Demi Lovato** is always smiling. That's very attractive in a girl. It makes her seem like she's never in a bad mood. It was what attracted me to my girlfriend."
–SOHRAB, 18

friendly playfulness

"**Ashley Tisdale** is cute and giggly. She's high-energy. It's the exact opposite of playing hard to get, and that's why I like it. I don't want to be confused about whether a girl likes me."
–STERLING, 18

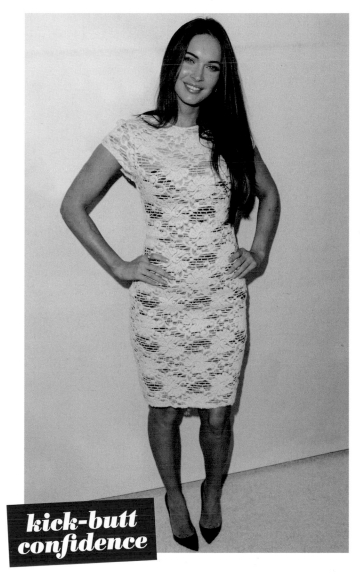

poise & charm

"Maybe it's the accent, but **Emma Watson** seems so graceful—she's the girl who walks into any room with her head up, and all the guys just stare."
–MICHAEL, 18

kick-butt confidence

"**Megan Fox** is a total babe. Part of it is the way she stands, with her shoulders back and her leg out. She exudes confidence."
–JOSH, 16

flirt
FROM ANYWHERE

No matter how many zillions of messages you get a day—whether it's a text or on Facebook—there's nothing like seeing your guy's name in your inbox. If the message is good, you'll read it out loud to your friends. If the message is great, you'll save it and read it when you're in a bad mood. And even if it just says "Hey, what's up?" you'll carefully plan each character of your reply. Ahead, guys weigh in on exactly what to send—and what not to—so that flirting becomes even more fun.

are your texts *hot or not?*

Find out what he'll think of your msg before you even hit send:

HOT!

INVITING HIM TO A PARTY

"Hanging out at Sarah's! Come now, bring friends."

This text makes it clear you're rounding up a group, so you can invite him without seeming too forward.

MISSING HIM

"What would we be doing if I was with u right now?"

He'll immediately think about kissing you (whether or not he admits it!). Save this one for a guy you're already seeing.

CALLING HIM TO THE RESCUE

"Need a homework break. Save me!"

This leaves it up to him to make the next move, whether it's sending you a few funny texts or asking you to hang out.

NOT!

ASKING FOR A RECAP

"How was ur weekend?"

Questions too broad to answer in 160 characters take too much effort to address. Stick to quick Qs ("Did u make it 2 the game?") so that he can send a fast reply.

CHECKING IN ON HIM

"Did u get my text?"

Unless your text was intercepted by the CIA, he got your message. If you want to nudge him, keep it jokey, so you don't seem annoying. ("My grandma texts faster than u!")

CALLING HIM OUT

"We need to talk."

You don't want your texts to feel like he's getting sent to the principal! He'll know you're ticked and feel a wave of dread about replying to you.

#17GuyQ

Q: How can I tell if a guy likes me?

A: "Readers ask me this question almost every day on Twitter! My response is usually, 'How much do you talk to each other?' The truth is, if you don't talk very often, then the guy probably doesn't like you. A guy who likes you will find excuses to talk to you, text you, and see you as much as possible—just like you would do to him. You won't feel confused about how he feels, because he'll want to make sure you're absolutely certain."
—ALEX

tricky text situations!

Staring blankly at your phone?
Not to worry—here's exactly what to say!

You have endless flirty text banter, but now you want to hang out in person.

ASK HIM OUT!

Next time he asks about your weekend, write back, "Crazy story! Coffee meet-up?" Being direct saves you from hours of dropping hints about hanging out. If he's not free, he'll know that it's his turn to make the next move.

He texts you nonstop all night—then goes MIA for days.

INITIATE A CONVO!

Don't wait to find out if he's interested—bring up something you talked about and see if he takes the bait: "Looked up that YouTube vid. So funny! Any other recs?" End with a question to prompt a fast response.

You finally got up the nerve to send a flirty text—and he sent back a dud one-word reply.

DO NOTHING!

His short response could mean he's over you or that he's just in the middle of something. Either way, you shouldn't have to do all the flirting work! So don't write anything back until he texts again—if he likes you, he will!

#17GuyQ

Q: I traded numbers with a cute guy at a party, then texted him the next day. He wrote back, 'Sorry, who is this?' It was awful! What should I have done?

A: "Let it slide! This text can feel like a rejection, but it's possible he just doesn't have your name saved in his phone. Write back, 'It's Hillary. We met last night. Does your phone have amnesia? ;)' You'll clue him in—without letting him off the hook entirely. Next time, jog his memory up front: 'Hey, it's Hil! We bonded over Cool Ranch Doritos ...'"
—TIM, 20

HIS WEIRD TEXTING BEHAVIORS, EXPLAINED

When his texts take a totally random turn, here's the message he's really trying to send:

HE TEXTS	HE MEANS
"Haha"	He doesn't have anything else to say and wants to end the conversation. Don't bother responding unless you hear from him again.
"You still at the party?"	If he's trying to find you at the end of the night, he wants to hook up. If you don't want a random makeout, wait until the morning to write back.
"Up to anything fun tonight?"	He might want to hang out, but he's not committing until he finds out if any of the other people he sent this mass text to respond with better plans.
"Text me later if you want to meet up."	Instead of making a plan to see you, he's making you do the work. Ignore him for now—he'll text again if he really wants to hang out.

your best *facebook* flirting moves

Three little ways to make him *really* "like" you

1

***make your status
an inside joke*** … and your secret
shout-out will become a cute way to stay
on his mind. Ignore the "???" comments
from your friends and wait for
his "like" to make the next move.

2

send a game request with the
message: "Loser buys pizza! ;)"
Sneakiest way ever to get a date!

3

create a Facebook event for an
impromptu Dunkin' Donuts run and
invite him and a few close friends. The
last-minute factor keeps things casual but
shows that he's in your inner FB circle.

IS HE A FB PLAYER?

**Find out if he likes you—
or is he just playing games:**

He has tons of friends.

If your guy has more than 1,000
friends, it's unlikely he actually knows
them all—he's probably sending requests
to every cute girl he knows. Ew.

He always changes his pic.

It's one thing to change your profile pic
when someone uploads a cute photo of
you. But a guy who posts a hot new photo
every other day is looking for attention
from all the girls on his friends list.

His profile is empty.

If a guy you're close to blocks you from
seeing his wall or his pics, he could
be hiding the evidence that there are
other girls in the picture—literally!

STATUS: IT'S COMPLICATED

Also, um, why are dudes so notoriously slow to change their status to "in a relationship"? They explain:

it doesn't mean anything!

"My girlfriend kept pestering me to change my status because she didn't want other girls to 'swoop in.' I changed it, but I couldn't drop the feeling that she didn't trust me, which led to our split. I was into her; I'm just not that into announcing it on Facebook!"

–James, 20

it's nobody's business!

"My girlfriend wanted to change our status to 'in a relationship,' but I said no. Our close friends know we're dating, so why do I need to tell hundreds of random friends? I don't like the world knowing details of my personal life, or hearing about it if we break up."

–Javey, 21

Q: What does it mean if my crush deletes my Facebook comments?

A: This is shady. He sounds like a player. He doesn't want other people to think that he's involved with you—probably because he wants to seem available to other girls. You should definitely take it as a sign to move on."

–RYAN

seventeen **HOT GUY** PANEL

41

decode

HIS FLIRTING MOVES!

Dude-behavior is one of the most confusing things on planet Earth, so instead of wasting hours with your friends analyzing every line in your Facebook convo with him, here's the breakdown on what he's actually trying to say!

read his
body language

These hot celeb guys are using their best moves.
Can you tell what they really mean?

AN INTENSE STARE

A guy who looks at you like **Austin Butler** is gazing at **Vanessa Hudgens** is lovestruck! Other clues? If he touches your knee or crosses his legs toward you.

A NECK GRAB

Holding you in a vulnerable spot in public is sketchy—like he's trying to get the upper hand. Are **Andrew Garfield** and **Emma Stone** headed for trouble?

THE FINGER LACE

Intertwined fingers and a tight grip are a sure sign of a super-close connection. These two couldn't be more in sync—**Joe Jonas** is smitten with **Blanda Eggenschwiler!**

"what a *crush* feels like for me!"

Yep, guys obsess over their every flirting move too. Here's proof:

i overanalyze!

"On the first day of class, this smokin' hot girl sat next to me. All these questions raced through my mind: Why did she sit next to me? Is she going to stay? What's she like? I tried to play it cool and introduce myself. Ever since then, every time she'd sit next to me, my pulse would race a little bit, and I'd hope something would happen."

–Cory, 19

i geek out!

"When I have a crush on a girl, I get really hot and I start to breathe a lot faster, which causes me to sweat. Then I get nervous because I'm sweating, but I try to cover it up with a joke or two."

–Neil, 19

i run game!

"When I talk to my crush, I don't feel nervous—it's a challenge. I never allow myself to think I can't get her. I keep my head high, act like I have dated hotter girls, and talk about other girls texting me to make her think she has competition—even if she doesn't."

–Doug, 18

i obsess!

"Every time I'm around my crush, my stomach is in knots, my brain turns to jelly, and I can't think of anything to say. Then I check Facebook every couple days to see if she's still single."

–Aaron, 16

GET TO KNOW...
CHRIS

AGE 20

RELATIONSHIP STATUS Single

CELEBRITY CRUSH Lucy Hale

HOW I LIKE TO BE PICKED UP "I like to be picked up by a girl who has confidence. Just a simple introduction ('Hey, I'm _____.') with a smile is all you need to do!"

THE BEST FLIRTING MOVE A GIRL HAS EVER TRIED ON ME "One time a girl 'accidentally' bumped into me. When I apologized, she said, 'You better make it up to me. Find me on the dance floor!' She made her presence known but still left it up to me to chase after her."

MY BIGGEST FLIRTING FAIL "One time at a party, I went up to the prettiest girl and said, 'Hi. The voices in my head told me to come over and talk to you.' She gave me the most freaked out look I've ever seen!"

what he's *really* trying to say

Understanding dude-speak does not have to be as tough as your Latin homework. Here's how to read between his lines!

HE SAYS	HE MEANS	WHY
"What are you doing this weekend?"	**"I want to see you, but I'm too nervous to ask."**	This shy guy is crossing his fingers that your convo will turn into **a chance to hang out.** Spare him the awkward small talk and say, "I've been craving IHOP. Want to go?" He'll love you for it!
"That guy is lame. Why are you into him?"	**"Why aren't you into *me*?"**	Hearing you gush about another dude **makes him feel competitive.** If he keeps finding reasons to diss the other guy in the future, that's more than just jealousy. He totally likes you!
"Who will be there?"	**"Some of your friends suck."**	Harsh truth—one of your friends **drives him crazy,** and he's already dreading spending time with her. Tell him to bring one of his friends, so he doesn't feel overridden by girl talk.
"Wanna just hang out at my house tonight?"	**"Let's hook up."**	This guy isn't inviting you over to watch a movie—he wants to **make out with you** until your parents call and tell you it's time to come home.
"The thing is, I don't really know what I want right now."	**"I'm not interested in you."**	By playing the "I'm trying to figure myself out" card, he's **avoiding the awkwardness** of saying that he doesn't want to get serious.

why he *didn't* make a move

You thought you two were hitting it off—and then he didn't ask for your number. Ugh! Here's why:

HE HAD BAD BREATH!

"I try to look my best, but if I think my breath might smell and don't have a mint, I wouldn't ever make a move."
–BRANDON, 19

HE'S INSECURE!

"When I feel like a girl is out of my league, like if she's really pretty with a great personality, it's difficult for me to approach her. It's intimidating and I become too shy to talk to her."
–JACOB, 19

HE WANTED THE UPPER HAND!

"I have a strict policy not to pursue girls. If they pursue me, it means they must really like me. So in my mind, there's a better chance things will actually last."
–MICHAEL, 20

YOU WERE TOO DISTRACTED!

"If a girl seems the least bit bored, I won't keep talking to her. I want her to feel as psyched about me as I do about her."
–DUSTIN, 21

YOU'RE SURROUNDED BY YOUR CLIQUE!

"Groups easily intimidate me. When I see a cute girl across the room, I want to talk to her—until I notice she has a wall of friends fencing her in."
–MATT, 20

YOUR FRIENDS ARE ANNOYING!

"You're usually similar to the people you hang out with, so if your friends get on my nerves, there's a good chance you might too."
–NICHOLAS, 19

WHY HE STOPPED CALLING

What's worse than not making a move at all? Making a move and then going totally MIA. Here's what he was too afraid to say to your face!

your wild side turned him off.

"I brought the girl I was dating to a house party. She got so drunk that she started sloppily flirting with everyone there, guys and *girls*. I felt like she'd morphed into a different person—from a sweet girl to a *Girls Gone Wild* girl. That was the last time we hung out."

–Ian, 20

he heard a nasty rumor.

"I thought the girl I was seeing seemed perfect—until a friend told me she'd cheated on her last boyfriend. It surprised me so much, I started doubting our connection. I couldn't shake the thought, 'That could be me.'"

–Harrison, 18

the kiss was a dud.

"After a few dates, I finally hooked up with the girl I was seeing. By the time I got home that night, I was over her. Without the anticipation of the hookup, it turned out I wasn't interested. We're still friends, but the chemistry just wasn't there."

–Jacob, 19

be a
SUPER-
DATER

GET THE
date!

You've totally hit it off at parties—but now you're ready for some flirty one-on-one time. What's the best way to make it happen? Check the pages ahead for easy ways to take your hangouts into date-zone, plus tons of "what to do" ideas that guys love and are guaranteed to make you look ultra-cool. Your best date ever is just around the corner!

SNEAKY WAYS
to ask *him* out
(without really asking!)

Inviting a guy to hang out is so weirdly formal, but there is a better way.

1
start small.

A date doesn't have to require tons of advance planning—just offer your guy a ride home. Once you're in the car, you can slip in a way to extend your time together. "I'm starving! Want to go to Shake Shack?" Suddenly you're flirting over French fries!

2
suggest crazy ideas.

Mention doing something out of the norm, so that it almost comes off as a dare. ("Should we wait in line for the midnight show?!?") No guy will back down from a challenge! Then say, "It would be fun! Let's do it for real!"

3
invite him to tag along.

Text your guy, "Going for a run later. Want to come?" When you're including him in plans you've already made—not arranging your sched around him—it makes the question seem totally casual. If he says no, whatever. You were going to do it anyway!

4
get his insight.

When he brings up the new speakers he's obsessed with, tell him you want to check them out sometime. Asking for his gadget wisdom gives you a chance to bond over something he's already into. Plus, guys love to be in the know!

what his *date idea* really means

There's a hidden message behind where he asks you to hang … and it's time to uncover it!

IF HE ASKS YOU TO…	**IT MEANS…**
bowl with friends	### HE'S NOT COMFORTABLE! "I'll ask my crush on a group date like bowling if I'm not ready to spend one-on-one time together. I want to know her better—but in a casual setting with little pressure, so it doesn't feel awkward." –Jay, 17
go to a concert	### HE'S TESTING YOU! "Concerts are a great place to bring a girl if I want to learn how fun she is. If she's smiling and dancing, I'll know she's the type who's up for going out and trying new things." –Glenn, 17
come to his game	### HE WANTS TO SHOW OFF! "When I invite a girl to watch one of my baseball games, it's because I like her enough to want to impress her. That, and I get to brag to my teammates that I have a cute girl in the stands!" –Lucas, 16
watch a movie at his place	### HE'S READY TO HOOK UP! "Asking a girl to come over to my house to watch a DVD means I want to make out! I'll choose a chick flick, so I can make a move by leaning in and kissing during the romantic parts." –Mark, 17

GET TO KNOW...
DAN

AGE 20

RELATIONSHIP STATUS Single

CELEBRITY CRUSH Jennifer Lawrence

THE BEST DATE I'VE EVER BEEN ON "About a year ago, I took a girl out on a hike and we watched the stars. It was simple, but we had the freedom to talk for hours, and by the end of the night, I felt like I'd gotten to know her really well."

HOW A GIRL CAN TELL IF I WANT TO KISS HER AT THE END OF THE NIGHT "I usually make a lot of eye contact, especially as the night winds down. And of course if I'm flirting a lot throughout the date, that's another sign that I'm hoping for a kiss later!"

"I'm quite old-fashioned. I like going out to dinner [on a date]. You have the chance to really get to know someone better."
–Harry Styles

weird things he does before a date

You'd never leave the house without one last mirror check—but you won't believe these guys' elaborate rituals!

PUMP MY EGO!

"I wink at myself in the mirror and say, 'You ready to go, Big Guy?'"
–DYLAN, 18

SPRITZ AWAY!

"When I'm getting ready for a date, I always hit my key spots with Axe: pits, chest, crotch, and butt. I just can't leave the house without smelling fresh. It's an awesome compliment when a girl says you smell good—it's like a hint that she's into you."
–BRIAN, 18

WORK OUT!

"Before any date, I do two sets of ten pull-ups so my arms swell up. It's the most important part of getting ready."
–CHRIS, 19

Get squeaky clean! "I like to make sure I'm fresh and clean. I even wash behind my ears like my mom used to tell me!"
–Justin Bieber

THE BIG
night

Your hair looks great … your makeup looks glowy … and your outfit makes you look like a bazillion bucks! You've done all the prepping you can do, but now's the fun part … actually being on a date with your crush! You're wondering how to impress him, and what kind of questions you should ask—here, guys answer all of that and more!

20 *ultimate* date ideas!

When you're both stumped on what to do, just check one of these super-fun ideas off your list.

1 ROCK CLIMBING!
Tackling that giant wall is a challenge (and a buzz). Going through it as a team is a major way to boost your energy.

THRILL-SEEKER SPOT!

2 A SPORTS GAME
"One night, my BF and I got cheap tickets to a local baseball game. We cheered all night and shared a cup of Dippin' Dots. It was a laid-back date, so we got to relax and be ourselves."
–TAVYA, 17,

3 A HIGH ROPES COURSE!
They're loaded with fun challenges like tightrope walking, rock-scrambling, and zip-lining—and on some of them, the only way to get across successfully is by working hand-in-hand with your partner.

5 A MUSEUM
"On our first date, my boyfriend and I didn't know what to do, so we went to an art museum. That's not usually my thing, but looking at the artwork gave us tons to talk about—and then afterward we found a bench in the gardens outside to watch the sunset!"
–ALEXANDRA, 17

6 A PLAYFUL PAINTBALL SESH.
Dodging opponents and marking hot guys before time runs out is as exciting as it gets! Bonus: Many locations offer special discounts, so hit up the web site before you go.

GROUP DATE IDEA!

7 A ROOFTOP PICNIC.
If the roof of your house is flat, spread a blanket on top of it. Then bring all of your favorite snacks to share!

8 A SCARY MOVIE!
When you're freaked out, your heart pumps faster, so it intensifies the nervous-in-a-good way feeling from being around someone you really like.

ADRENA-DATE!

9 BUILD-A-BEAR
"My date and I were walking around the mall. We passed the Build-a-Bear workshop and I made a joke about how I had always wanted to go growing up. He said, 'Want to go right now?' It was so fun to act like a kid: I picked out a monkey, and my guy got into choosing the clothes. We named him Elmer. It was random, but we had the best time!"
–CELESTINA, 18

10 A VIDEO GAME TOURNAMENT
Get a group of friends together for a Red Bull-fueled Wii Mario Kart tournament (and of course team up with your guy!).

4 GOING FOR ICE CREAM!
What's sweeter than separate cones? Tackling super-size sweets together, like the Chocolate Extreme Blizzard from DQ. Plus, a massive treat gives you the perfect excuse to linger a little longer.

DATE IDEAS FROM DUDES!

11 PLAY MINI GOLF!
"Playing a game takes away any awkwardness in the beginning. Plus, a little friendly competition shows off my upbeat personality."
—JOE

12 FIND THE BEST VIEW IN TOWN!
"For VDay, my girlfriend and I went to the top of the stock exchange building in Chicago, where you have an amazing view of the city. It was like something out of a romantic movie—and we made out, obviously."
—ZACH

13 HAVE AN OUTDOOR FOOD FEST!
"I love having a chill picnic in the park. That way we can relax and just focus on getting to know each other. We'd get a couple of crepes, and talk about everything!"
—GIUSEPPE

14 AN OUTDOOR CONCERT!
"A concert is a sweet date because there's no pressure to think about what to talk about. Then afterward you can recap together."
—BRETT

15 GO ICE-SKATING!
"If the girl needs to hold me for support, it gives us a chance to get close!"
—JARED

16 COOK DINNER TOGETHER!
"Grocery shopping with my girlfriend was so fun—we ran all over the store looking for ingredients and chased each other with carts. When we got home, we made a huge mess cooking and realized that we accidentally doubled one of the ingredients. Ha! But we were cracking up the whole time."
—ROB

17 SPEND A DAY AT THE AMUSEMENT PARK!
"In the summer, theme parks get particularly crowded, so I can pull the 'I'm holding your hand so we don't get separated' move."
—RYAN

18 PLAN A SURPRISE!
"My girlfriend said she wanted to take a walk in the snow, but as we were walking, she pulled me into a restaurant where she'd had a reservation all along! I was

so touched that she made the effort to surprise me."
—NIPUN

19 CUDDLE TO CORNY MOVIES.
"Run to Wal-Mart together for hot chocolate and a couple of DVDs from the $5 bin. They always have the most random selection, which makes it fun."
—ETHAN

20 WING IT!
"Sometimes no plan is the best plan! By having a date with no limits, we don't have to stress over any expectations for the night. We'd meet up and just see where the day takes us."
—ERNEST

totally hit it off on date night!

Pssst … here's how to avoid his biggest pet peeves!

if you're out to dinner…

ADORABLE! "I like when my date takes forever to decide what to order. Some guys would get impatient, but I like that it gives us time to talk."
–PAUL, 18

ANNOYING… "I kind of hate it if a girl complains about the food—especially if she chose the place! It makes me feel like I don't know how to show her a good time."
–COREY, 16

OH, JEEZ, NO! "A girl who does not thank me for paying is a snob. You don't have to offer to pay, but at least recognize I'm doing something nice."
–ZACHARY, 19

if you're at the movies…

ADORABLE! "It's cute when a girl moves closer to you and whispers a few comments. It shows that she's thinking about you."
–TOM, 17

ANNOYING… "Making shuffling noises in your seat during the movie is so annoying! I want to watch the movie, so it's distracting if you're fidgeting around."
–MICHAEL, 21

OH, JEEZ, NO! "If a movie starts at 7:15, it doesn't mean we leave your house at 7:15! I don't want to miss the movie because you're still checking yourself out. So yes, you look hot—now hurry up!"
–JOHN, 20

if you're at his place…

ADORABLE! "I love hanging out with a girl and just talking, especially when we disagree. It's great when she won't stop talking until her point is proven."
–XAVIER, 19

ANNOYING… "It's frustrating when a girl is always up for whatever I suggest we do. I want her to voice her opinion and have a say in our relationship."
–MATHEW, 20

OH, JEEZ, NO! "I get mad when I'm hanging out with a girl and she starts making fun of other people so she looks better. It's just not nice!"
–MIKE, 15

#17GuyQ

Q: How can I avoid an awkward silence on a date?

A: "A girl can never go wrong by bringing up sports or movies that have recently come out. When my girlfriend and I are out on a date, we love to look around and guess whether they are single, on a date, or married based on how they interact with each other. It's always entertaining and has sparked a lot of fun conversations! Whatever you do, don't resort to pulling out your phone on a date! That will just make him think you'd rather be doing something else."

–JACK, 21

don't stress about this stuff!

It's hard not to overthink things on a date, but these hotties don't want you to. Phew!

EATING A LOT

66It bothers me when girls won't eat in front of me. When you enjoy your food, it shows me that you're relaxed and having a good time!**99**
–SEAN, 20

A PRICEY OUTFIT

66It's good to look nice, but the convo matters much more than your clothes, especially on a first date. I'll remember what you said—not what you wore.**99**
–SAM, 18

A SUDDEN BURP

66No one should feel embarrassed by that—make a joke about it to show off your sense of humor!**99**
–DANIEL, 20

FADING MAKEUP

66I like when a girl doesn't wear makeup while she's hanging out with me. It shows that she feels comfortable, and that makes her even more attractive.**99**
–BRYAN, 19

his dating traumaramas

Real guys fess up to their most humiliating date snafus.

66 I went to Olive Garden with a girl I really liked, and I wanted her to be my first kiss. At the end of our meal, I leaned across the table to go in for it, but instead I knocked my water glass into her lap. 99
–JHAN, 17

66 I was supposed to meet this girl at the movies—but she never showed. Since I'd already paid, I just watched the movie alone. When I came out, there she was waiting for me. I felt too stupid to admit I'd messed up the times, so I bought two more tickets and watched it again. 99
–ANTHONY, 17

66 My date and I went to Burger King and ordered our meals. The total came to 15 bucks, so I pulled out my wallet—only to find the receipt for $20 headphones I'd bought earlier that day and forgotten about! So she had to pay. Oops! 99
–DARIN, 19

66 My date wanted to see this scary movie, so I tried to hide how freaked out I was. On our way out, we were almost at my car, when I heard someone running after me. I shrieked 'Ah!' and started sprinting. It turned out to be one of the employees chasing me down to return the wallet I dropped! 99
–PATRICK, 17

SO...
HOW'D IT GO?!

When you walk through the door after a date, it's like your body automatically goes from a super-charged adrenaline high to total exhale mode. You lie in bed and replay every last detail in your mind, and the crush on him you had before? Now it's TEN TIMES bigger! You know you had the best time ever ... but what's *he* thinking? Turn the page and find out.

decode your date!

Don't you wish you could predict from date one whether he's BF material? If you know how to read his secret signals, you can!

HE'S A KEEPER IF ...

he's a little bit awkward.

If he has obvious date jitters—like he has trouble making eye contact or asks small-talky questions—it's because you make him nervous. That's good! He sees going out with you as a big deal; you're not just any random girl.

he has a good relationship with his mom or sister.

He has spent more time with them than any other woman in his life—so if he answers Mom's calls while you're out or mentions some cute or funny detail about his sister, it's a sign he'll treat you with the same respect in the long run.

he teases you.

When a guy lightly pokes fun at you or calls you out on something goofy, it's proof that he's really paying attention—and that he is trying to break the ice so he can feel more comfortable around you. A little joking around is a good sign; you'll never get bored with a guy who makes you laugh.

he talks about himself.

No doubt it's annoying if a guy acts like Mr. Braggy B. McBraggington—but he may feel he needs to prove himself to win your approval. (It's actually kind of sweet!) As long as he balances his self-promotional monologue with questions about you, it's safe to assume he's showing off only to win your heart.

HE'S A GONER IF ...

he pours on the compliments.

You might feel flattered, but if he says stuff that seems generic ("You have beautiful eyes") or way too slick ("That dress is so sexy")—your playa-rader should start beeping. He is probably feeding the same lines to every girl.

he texts throughout the date.

Beware the chronic texter! If he's constantly sending messages (in the car, during dinner, etc.) while giving you distracted mmm-hmm responses in person, it's like he's saying, "You're okay for now, but this other person is more important." Later!

he's too touchy-feely.

It's nice when you know a guy is into you, but even if your tiniest inner voice is telling you he seems more physical than he should be (dude, it's the first date), trust your instincts. At the end of the night, he might want more than a hug.

he wants to get drunk or high.

It might seem thrilling to hang out with someone who acts like he's the life of the party. (And yeah, getting buzzed will make him way more confident and flirty, so it may seem like you're really hitting it off!) But by getting wasted, he is actually putting a wall between the two of you—like he's not willing to show you his true sober self. Next!

say the right thing!

Want to get your point across after a date? Here's your script:

IF YOU'D LIKE TO SEE HIM AGAIN...

Be light and flirty—not desperate!

SAY: *"You are so cute! Hanging out with you is always the best part of my [day/week/weekend]."*

....

IF YOU WANT TO TAKE IT SLOW...

Be clear—and don't apologize!

SAY: *"I'm the type of person who likes to have something to look forward to, so I tend to move more slowly."*

....

IF YOU'RE NOT THAT INTO HIM...

Be direct—don't leave any room for hope!

SAY: *"Thanks for the night out. Have a good one!"*

#17GuyQ

Q: What really goes through a guy's head at the end of a date?

A: "I'm probably just kicking myself for spilling something at dinner or being clumsy. At the same time, I just hope she likes me. If she stalls when we get back to her place, I'll go in for a kiss. It's nerve-racking, but I try to play it cool."
–GARRETT, 18

ARE YOU REALLY INTO THIS GUY?

It's easy to think you're into a guy who seems all that. But a smart dater needs to identify her true feelings.

DID YOU...

Have the feeling you could trust him to be alone in a room with your best friend and not argue, sit in total silence, or make a move on her?
You're INTO him!

Find yourself giving TMI nervously because there were lulls in conversation?
You're NOT into him!

Genuinely laugh at his jokes or attempts to make you laugh?
You're INTO him!

Get easily distracted while he was talking by pretty much everything going on around you?
You're NOT into him!

Picture yourself making out with him—or find yourself hoping that he'd make a move?
You're INTO him!

Censor yourself around him because you thought your opinions were dumb or would make him mad?
You're NOT into him!

SNEAKY WAYS
to *stay* on his mind!

Here's how to make sure he'll be thinking about you days after your date!

1
pay a big compliment.

You know how you always remember when someone tells you that you look like a celebrity? Use this tactic to your advantage by dropping in a specific compliment while you're hanging out. ("When you smile, you look so much like Channing Tatum! Do you get that a lot?") Just make sure the praise is sort of true, or it'll sound like a line.

2
bet on the future.

Steer the convo toward an upcoming event—like March Madness or the Super Bowl—and bet on how it'll turn out. When the game rolls around, he'll think of you (especially if you text a little trash talk his way!).

3
save your best story.

At the end of the night, tease him with a juicy nugget of info. ("Next time, remind me to tell you about my crazy spring break in Daytona.") He'll push you to spill, but wave him off and say, "Sorry—got to get inside! It's the kind of story that needs telling over cheese fries . . ." You're giving him a super-easy way to ask you out again!

4
snap a picture.

If you're on a group hangout, ask if he'll take a picture of you and a friend—then tell him to jump in the next shot. When you tag him on Facebook a few days later, comment with a cute question, "Nice pic … what's the secret to your swagger? ;)" He'll be enticed to respond!

YOUR SECRET POST-DATE WEAPON:

his friends!

When you're dating a new guy, it's key to warm up to his buddies, too. (Think about how much you value your BFF's opinions when it comes to your love life!) A guy never fully commits without his friends' stamp of approval, so how do you win them over without looking like you're trying too hard? These tricks will make them love you instantly!

cracking the bro code

First, you must know there are rules among guys that a bro must never break. What do they mean for *you?* Real guys explain.

NEVER BAD-MOUTH YOUR BRO.

66 A guy isn't allowed to say anything bad about his friend in front of cute girls—especially if he's the wingman for the night. When a guy starts trashing his friend to you, it means that he likes you—and he is trying to give himself a leg up on the competition. 99

–DIEGO, 20

PUT YOUR BRO PLANS FIRST.

66 A guy can't ditch his best friends for a girl when his bros are counting on him to be there. Don't ask your boyfriend to blow off his friends if he's had those plans for a while. It will definitely cause a fight! 99

–BRETT, 20

RESPECT YOUR BRO'S EX.

66 Guys won't date a friend's ex unless they have permission first. If a guy you like is friends with one of your past boyfriends and hasn't asked, he's waiting for the okay. 99

–PAXSON, 18

DON'T GROSS OUT YOUR BROS.

66 It's not cool to make out with your girlfriend in front of your bros. So don't be surprised if your guy isn't into PDA— he just doesn't want to make his friends feel uncomfortable. 99

–ERIC, 20

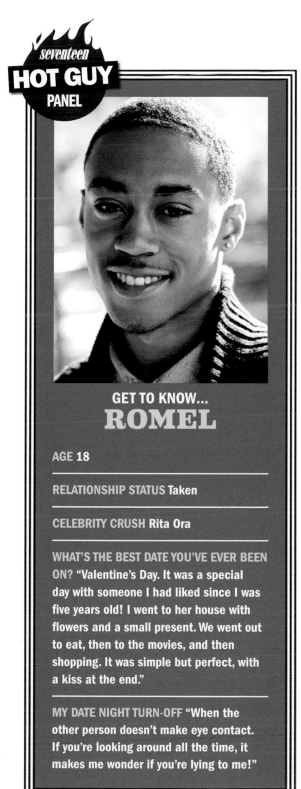

HOT GUY PANEL *seventeen*

GET TO KNOW...
ROMEL

AGE 18

RELATIONSHIP STATUS Taken

CELEBRITY CRUSH Rita Ora

WHAT'S THE BEST DATE YOU'VE EVER BEEN ON? "Valentine's Day. It was a special day with someone I had liked since I was five years old! I went to her house with flowers and a small present. We went out to eat, then to the movies, and then shopping. It was simple but perfect, with a kiss at the end."

MY DATE NIGHT TURN-OFF "When the other person doesn't make eye contact. If you're looking around all the time, it makes me wonder if you're lying to me!"

weird dude friend behaviors, *explained*

When your guy starts with the fart jokes and fist-bumping around his friends, you might question who he really is. Here's the dude truth!

the weirdness	the explanation
He goes from being chill with you to super-competitive about everything with them.	**WE'RE BONDING!** "Guys may let their guard down around girls, but around other guys, we want to prove that we're stronger/faster/better than everyone. Sure, competing over something like Halo has a friendly tone of joking around, but we're also really trying to outdo each other and be the best." **–EVAN, 20**
They rip on each other for being "so whipped," as if you're some kind of high-maintenance diva.	**WE'RE JEALOUS!** "When a guy starts spending a ton of time with his girl, we feel jealous that we're on the backburner—but instead of being mature enough to say, 'Dude, we miss you,' we just make fun of him. You shouldn't take it to heart. We're teasing him, not you!" **–MAT**
His friends talk him into the dumbest crap. (Pranks! Fireworks! Ahh!)	**WE'RE LOYAL!** If my friends want me to do something dangerous or stupid in front of a girl and I say no, it's like I'm picking her over them—so I always go along with the craziness. Just let it happen. It doesn't hurt you!" **–ROSS, 19**
With his boys, he talks about movies he wants to watch or his random hobbies–stuff that he never mentions to you!	**WE'RE SPARING YOU!** "There are some 'manly' things I talk about only with my friends—like the UFC fight I'm dying to see. I just assume that most girls don't care, the same way I don't care about what you bought at the mall. If you do care, tell him. He'll think you're his dream girl!" **–KENDALL**

UMM ... BUT WHAT IF HE'S BEING A TOTAL JERK IN FRONT OF HIS FRIENDS?!?

When your sweet, loving boyfriend disappears around other dudes (say it with us, UGH!), here are the twisted reasons why:

HE'S...

getting respect

"If you're too sweet to your girl in front of your friends, she'll think she owns you. And when a guy doesn't stick up for himself, his girl can get too comfortable and lose respect for him."

–Chase, 18

being an a**

"A guy wants to be the alpha dog of the pack. A girlfriend once said something stupid, and I called her a loser to the amusement of my friends. It showed I was still one of them—even with a girl."

–Tony, 19

trying to impress you

"There's an unsaid competition that exists among guys for a girl's attention. By looking like 'the man' in front of his friends, a guy thinks he will appear more attractive to a girl."

–Justin, 20

playing games

"Guys think it makes a girl want them more if we show we don't care too much about her. It's a guys way of playing hard to get."

–Ray, 20

get *closer* with his guy friends

Now that you understand how your crush's friends think, here's how to win them over once and for all!

GO SOLO

"It's awesome when a girl hangs out with the guys even when her boyfriend isn't around. Create a relationship with all of us—not just him—and we'll look out for you."

–ALEX, 18

GIVE HIM SPACE

"A girl should be cool with 'guy time.' Let him go off and do his own thing for a few hours with his friends. That way we won't feel like you're taking him away from us."

–DIMITRI, 21

SHARE THE LOVE

"My girlfriend sends me and my college roommates care packages filled with food and DVDs. Involve his friends with simple acts like that and you're in."

–BOBBY, 19

KEEP HIS SECRETS

"Don't bring up any difficult issues he may be dealing with (like relationship problems!). He may not have told us, and then we'll all feel uncomfortable."

–DAVID, 23

DON'T PLAY DUMB

"It isn't attractive when the girl you're showing off plays the ditzy/silly card. Make an effort to be mature. Guys want to introduce a smart girl to their friends."

–TIM, 23

TALK THE TALK

"Being able to discuss stuff we're into, like sports or movies, makes you look fun and intelligent. Ask questions if you need to, so you can at least get into the convo."

–OWEN, 18

SUPPORT HIM

"Don't knock down your guy in front of us. It's one thing for me to rag on him, but if you join in, you'll come off as disloyal—not the type of girl I'd pick for him."

–BRANDON, 19

FACEBOOK CHAT THEM

"It's really cool when a girl checks in with her boyfriend's friends online. Going out of your way to say, 'Hey, what's up?' will show you care. Just don't get too flirty."

–ZACH, 17

JERK ALERT!

"If my girl looks really hot in a bikini, that'll gain my friends' approval. I mean, how can you not stare at a gorgeous girl laying out in her swimsuit?"

–AJAMU, 21

were you invited out with the guys?

Sometimes your guy is too nice to admit he doesn't want you to invade his friend time—so here's the real way to tell.

he says ...	translation
"Oh, do you want to come?"	He doesn't want you to come—or he would have invited you to join sooner.
"I thought you were hanging out with Jen?"	He feels bad about leaving you out, so he's trying to hopefully suggest alternate plans—so you're not forced to jump on his!
"It's mainly the guys tonight."	Don't make me look like the lame-o who's attached at the hip to his girlfriend!

what *he says* when you aren't around...

You tell your girls everything about your guy.
Here's how much he really shares about you!

HE THINKS HE'S IN LOVE!

"My buddy has crushed on this girl for years, and she recently decided she has feelings for him too. Now he can't stop talking about it! He brings her up for no reason, tells me every conversation they have, and wants my opinion on everything she says. I'm like, 'Dude, relax—you're going to seem desperate!'"

–JAMES, 20

HE'S CLUELESS ABOUT KISSING!

"My friend asked me how he can make out with his girl at a party to seem smooth. I told him to try the 'over the shoulder' makeout when he's dancing. Then you can always turn her around and kiss face-to-face. I'm worried he might screw it up since he's only a freshman, but I had to try."

–MATTHEW, 20

HE MAKES UP STORIES!

"When it comes to girls, there's a lot of exaggerating. Like my friend will say he had sex with a girl for three hours, but that could mean they had a random kiss at a party. It's the 'man complex'— you always want to impress your friends. If it gets around to everyone else, that's even better."

–CARSON, 21

WTF?!? HE WANTS TO RANK YOU!

"After one of my friends introduces us to his girl, he'll ask, 'Do you think she's hot?' Then we rate her on a scale from 1 to 10, but it really is about how she comes across personality-wise, not just looks. Guys ask because they're competitive— it's an ego boost to think, I'm dating this girl and everyone thinks she's a 10, and his girl is only a 7½."

–COLIN, 20

have
the best
MAKEOUT

BE A *kissing* EXPERT!

It could be your first kiss or your 100th. No matter how long you've been with your guy, there are super-easy ways to make every lip-lock tingle down to your toes. Let guys share the inside scoop on every little detail of an amazing kiss—and by the time you're finished reading their secrets, you should consider yourself fully prepped for a mind-blowing makeout marathon!

SNEAKY WAYS

to tell if he'll be a *good kisser!*

Before you think about your moves, here's how to tell if he's even at your level!

1 *he uses chapstick.*

Guys with chapped lips might be able to pull off a decent kiss, but making out is much more fun for you when he has super-smooth lips. Every time he slicks on the balm, he's paying attention to how his lips feel—so he'll be conscious of how they make you feel too!

2 *he chews gum a lot.*

He could be the most amazing kisser in the world, but hooking up will suck if he has bad breath. If your crush keeps gum in his locker or pops in a mint after lunch, he cares about how his mouth tastes—and he probably takes pride in his kissing rep!

3 *he takes his time.*

If he's too eager to kiss you, that means he might get too aggressive with his tongue. Look for a guy who doesn't rush through dates or seem like he's in a big hurry to get you alone. He'll care more about having a great kissing experience than just satisfying his urge to make out!

4 *he's a great dancer.*

A dude with hot moves on the dance floor has learned how to control his body. This means he won't be awkward when making out—he'll know exactly how to tilt his head, pull you close to him, and use his lips to really wow you.

have the
ultimate makeout

When his eyes get that soft focus and
the conversation trails off, here's exactly what to do with...

... *your EYES*

**IF YOU'RE A
BEGINNER**

Keep eye contact
until right before your
lips touch—it helps
build excitement. If
staring creeps you out,
look at the point
between his eyes. He
won't be able to tell!

**IF YOU'RE AN
EXPERT**

Leave your eyes open.
Watching each other
kiss is very intimate,
so it will make your
connection even
stronger—it's as if
you're both saying,
"Isn't this hot?"

... *your LIPS*

**IF YOU'RE A
BEGINNER**

On the lean-in, turn
your head ten degrees,
open your mouth
slightly, and aim for
his lower lip. Give it a
little squeeze with your
lips, then close them
again as you pull away.

**IF YOU'RE AN
EXPERT**

Try kissing his top lip
or the corners of his
mouth. When you get
adventurous, it shows
you're comfortable
and having fun, which
makes him more
adventurous too.

... *your TONGUE*

**IF YOU'RE A
BEGINNER**

Nothing! With a short
kiss, tongue is over-
kill. But as the kisses
start to build in pres-
sure, gently run your
tongue across his
bottom lip—it's a flirty
way to ease into it.

**IF YOU'RE AN
EXPERT**

Imagine making a "T"
with the tip of your
tongues: If he moves
his to the side, try to
cross it with yours. It
will help you respond
to what he's doing and
build up a rhythm.

... *your HANDS*

**IF YOU'RE A
BEGINNER**

Grab his hand and
intertwine your fingers.
It's a sweet move
that stops him from
getting grope-y and
keeps him focused
on what he's doing
with his lips!

**IF YOU'RE AN
EXPERT**

Reach for the back
of his head and gently
tousle his hair. Guys
love this—it's a super-
sensitive spot he's
not used to having
touched, so you'll
literally give him chills!

steamy vs. snoozy

Once you've got your go-to moves down,
these guys know how to *keep* kissing fun!

	LIPS	**TONGUE**	**HANDS**
snoozy	**FOLLOWING HIS LEAD** "A girl who seems like she's only responding to my kisses—instead of initiating them—gets old after a while." **–MELVIN, 20,**	**USING A GIMMICK** "I've heard people say you should spell out the alphabet with your tongue—but if you're just following a preset pattern, you're not paying attention to the other person." **–JOSH, 19**	**ELEMENTARY MOVES** "Putting your hands on his sides and leaving them there is awkward—it's not a slow dance at prom!" **–NICK, 21**
steamy	**BEING SPONTANEOUS** "Kiss an unexpected place, like his collarbone, forehead, or even the palm of his hand. I like to be surprised by the softness of a girl's lips!" **–MELVIN, 20**	**A GENTLE MASSAGE** "Massage his tongue with yours, or suck on his tongue while you make out. You have to get into a rhythm and let the passion of the kiss happen naturally!" **–JOSH, 19**	**TAKING INITIATIVE** "Brush your hand against his cheek, or run your fingers through his hair—it makes it seem like you're really into the moment and want to get even closer." **–NICK, 21**

Q: How do I know if he thinks I'm a good kisser without asking?

A: "It's all about the lean-in. If your guy leans into you, that means he's passionate about kissing you and can't get enough! If you're doing the leaning, you might need to add a little more sizzle."
—JACOB, 18

101

"omg!" hookups

Warning: for bold kissers only! The boyfriends of *Seventeen* readers reveal what they really think about these four out-of-the-box smooches:

the BUTTERFLY kiss

"When you're kissing your guy, change things up: Pull away and flutter your eyelashes against his cheek or temple."
—KERI, 22

WHAT HER BF THOUGHT: "This kiss was very romantic and gentle. It gave a typical makeout a more intimate feel. I definitely got shivers during the butterfly part. After the first time, I was like, let's do it again!"
—COLIN, 21

MAKEOUT METER:

the ICE CUBE kiss

"Put an ice cube in your mouth for one minute, then kiss. It feels great because his mouth is hot, and yours is so cold!"
—LAUREN, 18

WHAT HER BF THOUGHT: "This was awesome—as cold and refreshing as a snow cone. It would be even more interesting with a cherry Popsicle! Try it after you've dated for a while, because the hot/cold sensation is intense."
—GUTHRIE, 18

MAKEOUT METER:

the BLINDFOLD kiss

"I loosely tied my scarf around my boyfriend's eyes, gave him a few light kisses on his cheek, and then moved to his forehead and his mouth."
—HANNAH, 16

WHAT HER BF THOUGHT: "At first I didn't know what she was doing, but I liked not knowing where she was going to kiss me next. I loved when she finally kissed me on the lips! French kissing would make it even better!"
—TRAVIS, 16

MAKEOUT METER:

the HIDE-AND-SEEK kiss

"I hid a mint in the back of my mouth, then challenged my guy to get it out! Use a small mint because it is harder to find, and will keep the game going!"
—LAUREN, 21

WHAT HER BF THOUGHT:"I loved that there was a lot of tongue. I've never had my tongue brush against the inside of Lauren's cheek before, and it was amazing! Plus, it wasn't over quickly—the intensity kept building."
—JACOB, 20

MAKEOUT METER:

are you a *good kisser?*

Check everything that applies to you:

☐ You put on a conditioning lip balm at the beginning of the night, so by kiss time your lips are soft without being sticky.

☐ When you kiss someone new, you start with small close-lipped kisses, so you can match your guy's pace.

☐ Instead of keeping your hands at your sides, you experiment with ruffling his hair or gently tracing your fingers down his arm.

☐ You're not afraid to give subtle suggestions, like, "I love when your kisses are super-soft."

☐ You think it's fun to try new techniques, like moving your tongue in a different way.

☐ You don't try to plan your next move in advance—you let yourself stop thinking about the kiss and go with the flow.

....

BOTTOM LINE: The more signs you marked, the better a kisser you are. But the real key is not to think too much—just be aware of your body, his body, and what you feel. If you enjoy it, he will too!

seventeen
HOT GUY
PANEL

GET TO KNOW...
GIUSEPPE

AGE 21

RELATIONSHIP STATUS Single

CELEBRITY CRUSH Kendall Jenner

MY BEST KISS EVER "My date and I were dancing at a friend's party. At one point she just grabbed my head and kissed me. It showed me that she really goes after what she wants, which was so hot!"

THE BIGGEST TURN-ONS FOR A GUY ARE "Confidence (aka when girls do what they want instead of following the crowd!), a soft touch on the arm, and I love when a girl's hair smells nice!"

WHAT NOT TO DO DURING A HOOKUP "Do NOT chew gum while making out! One time I kissed a girl who was ... and somehow it ended up in my mouth! I like sharing things with my girl, but the same piece of gum is just too much!"

what's your *smooch* style?

Which kiss gets your heart racing? Your answer tells all!

gentle caress

Kevin Jonas & Danielle Deleasa

SWEET! To you, a great kiss is so romantic and melt-y that it makes time stand still. Try planting a trail of slow, tender pecks from your guy's ear to his lips—it will make the moment last forever.

full body embrace

Ashley Tisdale & Christopher French

SEXY! You love pulling out your hottest moves—it's a thrill to know you're wowing him! Halfway into a makeout, run your lips across the soft skin on his neck. He'll melt instantly.

carefree moment

Naya Rivera & Big Sean

FUN! You think kisses are like a present: an amazing surprise! Try brushing your lips across his—without kissing him—and then pause to give him a flirty look. A little tease is deliciously playful.

what *your kiss* says about you!

Your Cupid's bow (the indent on the top of your upper lip)
can reveal what you really need in a hookup!)

**APPLY LIPSTICK
AND KISS HERE!**

EXTREME

You're a total drama queen!
17 TIP: You tend to be a
no-holds-barred kisser, so
look for a guy who's just as
adventurous—or you'll be
bored in a second!

SLIGHT

You always keep your cool!
17 TIP: Not even a steamy
makeout makes you lose
control. Your secret weapon is
knowing it's hot to leave your
guy wanting more!

NONE

You know what you want!
17 TIP: When it comes to
hookups, avoid shy dudes
who won't make the first
move. You need a guy who's
super-confident too!

what *his moves* really mean

His hookup action can reveal more than you think. The clues to look out for:

HIS MOVE	WHAT IT MEANS	WHY HE DOES IT
he slowly kisses your neck.	*he's trying to impress you!*	"When I kiss her neck, I'm trying to show her that I'm fun to make out with—and hoping that makes me more attractive!" —ROBERT, 17
he gives you a peck on the cheek.	*you make him nervous!*	"If I kiss a girl on the cheek, it means one of two things: I don't want to risk moving too fast, or I'm afraid to make a real first move!" —MIKE, 17
he sucks on your bottom lip.	*he feels comfortable with you!*	"That means I'm finally relaxed enough around you to try new things. I won't rush into the lip bite—I've probably been waiting a while to kiss you like that!" —JORDAN, 17
he holds your chin.	*he's not that into it!*	"If I'm not clicking with a girl but still want to make out, I'll go in for a kiss and hold one hand on her chin. That way, I can control how long the kiss lasts." —ADAM, 18

be his *best* kiss!

Real guys confess their favorite moves. Ever.

leading with your eyes

"Your eyes are your best weapon. If we're making eye contact and you break it to look down at my lips, I know you want a kiss."

–Ryan, 20

touching his neck

"I love when a girl strokes the back of my neck. It's a sensitive spot, and it gets me thinking that maybe she'll kiss me there too!"

–James, 18

making him work

"Use amazing gum, and be a little bit teasing, like pull away when I'm starting to get into it. That's sexy, when you play hard to get!"

–Aaron, 17

drawing him in

"I love when a girl puts her hands on my face and pulls me closer. It makes me feel like she's into the kiss—and it's intimate, which is hot."

–Eric, 21

coming in close

"Take advantage of a loud party as an excuse to get extra close and talk into his ear. You'll make it irresistibly easy for him to kiss you."

–Randy

teasing him

"One time I went in for a kiss and a girl pulled back and gave me a flirtatious grin—like a mini rejection. Trust me, a little teasing is very hot."

–Paul, 18

lingering just a little

"Send the right signals: Lean into me at the movies or let a good-night hug last a second too long. That's like a green light for me to kiss you!"

–Matt

#17GuyQ

Q: When is the right moment to use tongue?

A: "After you've been making out for a bit, slowly move your tongue into his mouth, working your way up to more passionate kissing. Just don't move it around too fast—that can get weird and slobbery."
—GREG, 19

Nibbling his lip! "I love it when my girlfriend gives me a light, soft bite right on the lips."
—Tyler Posey

kissing
traumaramas!

Think you've had an embarrassing kissuation? Wait until you hear what happened to these guys!

 VAMPIRE DIARIES

66 I was hanging out with my buddy, and we invited two girls who were best friends over to his dorm. He was already interested in one of them and started making out with her pretty quickly, so I was left awkwardly trying to talk to the other one. Eventually I just went for it, and things got pretty hot. Everything seemed fine until they went to the bathroom together, and I heard screaming from out in the hall, 'OMG WHAT HAPPENED TO YOUR NECK!?!' Apparently I had left a bruise that covered half her neck. I was known as 'The Vampire' for about a month and never heard from her again. 99
–TOM, 22

LIP-LOCK!

66 One night, we were playing spin the bottle, and during my turn it pointed me to a girl with braces. I didn't think anything of it at first, but when I went in for it, my lips got stuck! 99
–HUNTER, 18

CAUGHT ON CAMERA!

66 One time, this girl and I were having a hot makeout in the stands at a school sporting event. Of course, someone with a video camera for the yearbook was panning the stands, and now it's in the video yearbook permanently. 99
–RYAN, 19

SO SNOT HOT!

66 This girl and I had been hanging out, and I was about to kiss her for the first time. It was cold out and my nose was running, and when I bent down to kiss her, a wad of snot landed on her nose! 99
–SHANE, 19

FOUL PLAY!

66 I was on the men's soccer team in high school, and one day, while we were stretching before a game, my teammate and I both leaned down at the same time and we accidentally kissed! GROSS! 99
–ANDREW, 21

YOUR *hookup* MASTER CLASS

The chemistry between you and your guy is so intense, you can hardly think of anything real to compare it to. Being with your guy is the best feeling in the world … but it can also be super-complicated! There's no time when you'd rather peek into a guy's brain than during—and after—a hookup, so here, dudes get real and go there. Learn their steamy thoughts—that way you can make smart moves every time!

how *he feels* about hooking up

Real guys break down every deet you need to know.

WHAT DO YOU CONSIDER "HOOKING UP"?

MOST GUYS SAY

making out

"My friends assume when you say hooked up, that means you kissed. If you did do more, you would definitely say so!"
–BILLY, 20

....

HOW LONG WOULD YOU WAIT?

MOST GUYS SAY

that night!

"If I hit it off with a girl, I'd have no problem kissing her that night. I'd hate to miss my chance to be with her!"
–RYAN, 19

....

HOW FAR WOULD YOU GO THE FIRST TIME?

MOST GUYS SAY

just kissing!

"Kissing isn't a big deal. It's when you go further that you form an emotional attachment. I won't cross that line so quickly!"
–TODD, 20

GET TO KNOW...
JOE

AGE 21

RELATIONSHIP STATUS Single

CELEBRITY CRUSH Anna Kendrick

MY BEST KISS EVER "My best kiss was with a girl I had liked for a while but never had the opportunity to be around a lot. When it finally happened, it was just something that felt long overdue, but worth the wait!"

THE BIGGEST TURN-ONS FOR A GUY ARE "Being able to joke around sometimes, a cute smile, and an adventurous personality!"

WHAT NOT TO DO DURING A HOOKUP "Don't overthink things! Just do what feels natural ... but remember that it's a good thing to smile and show him that you're having fun!"

his makeout
rule book

Who does he want to get with and how far will he go?
Guys confess their secret rules.

RULE 1
NO GOSSIP!

"My rule is to say as little as possible. Whenever my guy friends brag about a hookup, I can't help thinking how terrible the girl would feel if it got back to her … and since I go to a small school, it's likely that it will. No one else's business!"

–DENNY, 21

RULE 2
DIBS EXPIRE AFTER TWO MONTHS!

"If I want to hook up with a friend's ex, I wait until two months after they broke up—then she's fair game! That's enough time for my buddy to snap out of it. The only exception is if she broke his heart, then I wait four months—to be fair to him."

–ANTHONY, 19

RULE 3
NO OVERLAP!

"Last year I was hooking up with two girls. They were different class years, so I didn't think they'd find out about each other. But I began feeling so guilty that I broke things off with both of them. New rule: No overlapping!"

–NICK, 21

RULE 4
TEST HER WITH A KISS!

"A hookup is your chance to see if you have feelings for a person, so the first time, I never go past kissing—that's all it takes to tell if you click."

–CONRAD, 17

RULE 5
KEEP IT FRESH!

"Whenever there's a chance I might hook up, I buy a fresh pack of gum—just to be safe!"

–AARON, 17

RULE 6
THREE HICKEYS, YOU'RE OUT!

"If a girl gives me more than three hickeys in one night, I'm not going to call her again—it basically means she's slutty!"

–ALEX, 21

HOOKUP SIGNALS HE'S TRYING TO SEND YOU

His sexy moves reveal a deeper message. Make sure you get it!

Brushing your hair aside:
"I WANT TO KISS YOU"

"When all I can think about is kissing a girl, I'll brush her hair off her face to make sure nothing gets in our way. If she wants to take the hint and lean in first, even better!"

–Andrew, 20

Kissing your ear:
"I WANT TO GO FURTHER"

"If I've been kissing a girl for a while and I want to move things forward, I'll start kissing her ear. Ears are great turn-on spots, so they up the excitement and let her know I'm ready for the next step."

–Gerald, 19

Kissing your forehead:
"I'M DONE NOW!"

"Sometimes my girlfriend forgets I'm fine with just cuddling. Whenever I kiss her forehead instead of her lips, it's because I want to take a break from making out and just relax next to her."

–Stephen, 19

Being fidgety:
"I'M NOT INTO YOU"

"This one girl I hooked up with was way too aggressive—she kept climbing on top of me! Every time I'd stop the action and readjust, but she didn't tone it down. It made her seem clueless."

–Allan, 17

his *wild* in-the-moment thoughts!

You *think* you know what's going through his head, but there's more in there than you can imagine…

66Every time I kiss someone new, I think, Wow, I can't believe this is happening. I feel lucky and surprised.99 **–ANTON, 18**

66Sometimes I panic. Will it be awkward when we see each other at school? Could this be the start of a relationship? So many questions run through my brain so that it can be hard to enjoy the moment.99 **–REHAN, 17**

66With a girl I really like, I'm totally concerned about making things fun for her. I wonder, Am I doing this right? Is she enjoying it? What can I do to spice things up?99 **–NICK, 18**

66I think a lot about tongue. I've had girls shove their entire tongues in my mouth and it's gross, so I'm careful not to do that to anyone else!99 **–BOBBY, 17**

66The number one thing I'm thinking about is my breath—like, Wait, what did I have for dinner again? I've learned to keep mints on me so I don't feel paranoid!99 **–JIN, 19**

66I immediately start thinking about how I can get to the next step—making out is nice, but I want more. I spend most of my brain power thinking of clever lines that will help me get to home base.99 **–WILLIAM, 19**

66In the middle of a hookup, I secretly rate how hot the girl is, so I can decide whether it's worth bragging about to my friends in the morning.99 **–RILEY, 20**

#17GuyQ

Q: How can I tell during a hookup if he's into it?

A: "The whole experience is nerve-wracking, but the first thing that goes through my head is, Is this really happening?!? I'm finally getting to see what it's like to be with her. If there's chemistry between us, I'm thinking, Wow, this is great! My heart is racing and my mind is going crazy—I feel like I'm going 120 mph on a roller coaster. If there isn't that spark, I'm thinking, Ugh, what do I do now? Then I start thinking about ways to cut things short without looking like a jerk."
—LUKE, 20

you hooked up...
now what?

The official protocol, dispatched straight from dudes:

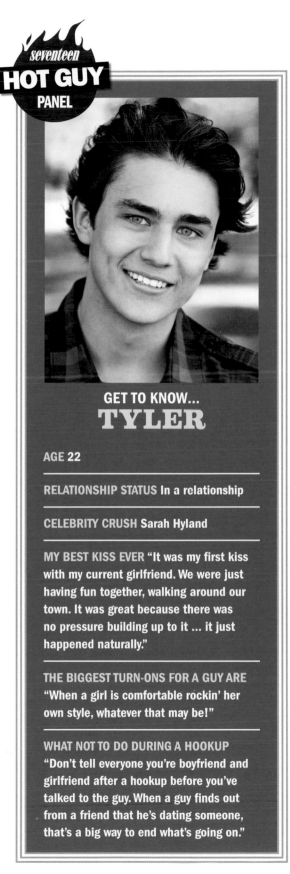

GET TO KNOW...
TYLER

AGE 22

RELATIONSHIP STATUS In a relationship

CELEBRITY CRUSH Sarah Hyland

MY BEST KISS EVER "It was my first kiss with my current girlfriend. We were just having fun together, walking around our town. It was great because there was no pressure building up to it ... it just happened naturally."

THE BIGGEST TURN-ONS FOR A GUY ARE "When a girl is comfortable rockin' her own style, whatever that may be!"

WHAT NOT TO DO DURING A HOOKUP "Don't tell everyone you're boyfriend and girlfriend after a hookup before you've talked to the guy. When a guy finds out from a friend that he's dating someone, that's a big way to end what's going on."

who should make contact first?

68%
OF GUYS SAY:
HE SHOULD!

"Girls overanalyze things, so the guy should make the first move to call her—that way, she's completely sure that he really does like her!"
–JAKOB, 21

should he call or text?

64%
OF GUYS SAY:
CALL!

"If the hookup is good, I'll call the girl, so I can tell her how much I enjoyed hanging out with her. She'll hear the excitement in my voice!"
–DANIEL, 20

make your hookup even *hotter!*

Sure, your moves are good—but are they on fire?
The Hot Guy Panel tells you tricks that turn up the heat.

"The first time you kiss, you barely touch his lips—just enough to give him a tiny bit of temptation." **-MAT**

"You pause to run your hands through your hair. It's like an invitation for a guy to touch it, too." **-CRAIG**

"When you're flirting, you tell him exactly what you want, like: 'Just kiss me already!' Then he knows for sure that you want him, too." **-KENDALL**

"At the end of the kiss, you look deep into his eyes, as if you're replaying every moment." **-MORGAN**

"You pull away for a minute and kiss his neck. That's the kind of move that makes me tingle all over." **-JOHN**

"You use your hands to pull his head toward you, as if you want to bring him as close as possible." **-HECTOR**

"You bite my lip gently and wrestle tongues. Playfulness is extremely sexy." **-MAC**

"You spice it up: Scratch his back a little, or just graze your hands all over his body." **-JUSTUS**

his secret makeout *stress!*

Think you're nervous about hooking up with a new guy?
Listen to what these dudes freak out about!

HIS STRESS

major drool

"I start to wonder if I'm getting slobbery! The worst kiss of my life was when a girl stuck her drooly tongue down my throat, so I'm paranoid about being bad for anyone else."

–AUSTIN, 18

HIS STRESS

her ex-boyfriend

"I notice if she's a better kisser than I am. If she is, I assume it's because her ex-boyfriend was a better kisser than me and taught her a thing or two about making out. And then I suddenly worry that I won't measure up!"

–ERIC, 20

HIS STRESS

bad breath

"I especially stress over what I ate, my breath, and how I smell! Every guy wants to make a good impression and not gross the girl out!"

–BRETT, 18

HIS STRESS

seeming too eager

"Once I got caught up in the passion of the moment, and I took off my shirt. I thought it was sexy, but the girl just looked at me like, 'What are you doing?' When she went to the bathroom, I put my clothes back on."

–SANDERS, 21

OMG! "I get so scared of getting a boner because it could freak the girl out! Girls are so lucky they don't have to worry about that. I always turn the lights off, so she can't see!"
–TOM, 21

his *weird kissing* behaviors, explained

No more freaking over what he said. Here's the final word on his WTF-moves

THE WEIRDNESS	THE EXPLANATION
after a few hook-ups, he suddenly goes MIA.	### his feelings changed. "Guys can be extremely passionate in the moment, but after the hormones fade, we step back and think, Did I really want that to happen? If he's not feeling it anymore, he'll drop off the face of the earth and avoid having to turn you down in person." **–Mac** 
he seems to like kissing, but the makeout never goes any further.	### he really likes you. "The idea that guys always want action is a stereotype. If he likes you, he'll want to take things slowly and build a relationship that's more than just physical stuff. It's a good thing!" **–Mitch, 19**
he flirts with me all night, then he doesn't try to make a move.	### he's on the fence. "There are two possibilities: He's either just into the thrill of the chase, or he's shy. Your best bet is to tone down the flirting. If he wants a chase, it will keep him intrigued. If he's nervous, he'll feel less intimidated. Either way, you win!" **–Justus** 
he's dated other girls before, but he's still a slobbery kisser!	### he's clueless! "Don't assume that he knows what he's doing just because he's 'experienced.' Pinpoint one thing you don't like about kissing and say, 'Try this instead . . .' He just needs a coach who can guide him without shattering his ego!" **–Diydan, 18**

defining the

RELATION

SHIP

falling
FOR HIM

Finding the right guy is better than eating mounds of chocolate, acing a test, or winning the last game of the season! But as amazing as that over-the-moon feeling feels like, it can also be seriously confusing. You know if your guy gives you major butterflies, but how do you know if you're truly in deep? Consider this your complete guide to figuring out what it feels like to fall in love—for real.

SNEAKY WAYS
to *define* the relationship

So are you together or not?
Skip "The Talk" and make DTR-ing stress-free!

1
pretend your BFF asked.

Everyone is wondering what the deal is between you two, so turn their nosiness into a good thing. Casually say to him, "My friends keep asking what's going on between us. What should I tell them?" It's a smooth way to get him thinking about it!

2
take your hangouts public.

If all you two do is watch movies at his place, it can be hard to figure out where you stand. Invite him out with other friends in couples. He'll either step up and act like you guys are one too, or he won't. Either way, you'll be clearer on your status!

3
open up about everything else.

When you both feel comfortable sharing deep stuff, you're moving into relationship territory. Next time your convo gets intimate, ease into DTR-mode by telling him how important he is to you. If he's feeling open, he'll respond with his thoughts about you.

4
schedule a way-later date.

Start talking about exciting plans down the road, as in, "Drake is coming to town—let's get tix!" If he's committed to hanging out with you four months from now, he's committed to *you.*

why he *doesn't* want to be official

When he pulls the "I'm not into labels" card, this is what he's really trying to say:

makes sense

HE DOESN'T WANT TO GET HURT.
"My last relationship ended badly, and it's made me think twice about getting serious with anyone new. When you keep things casual, it's safer—either of you could walk away at any minute." –DAN, 18

HE THINKS YOU'RE NOT INTO IT.
"I really liked this one girl who would flirt with me all the time—then turn around and flirt with my friends. At first it made her seem sexy, but by the time she decided she was into me, I was over it. I want a girl who wants me and only me. I won't commit if I think she's unsure." –MAX, 18

HE THOUGHT YOU WERE FRIENDS WITH BENEFITS.
"I was really good friends with this girl who I started hooking up with. But when she began talking about our future, I realized it was a mistake. I just couldn't get on the same page—I still saw her as a friend." –ZACH, 21

HE JUST WANTS THE CHASE.
"There was this one girl who always blew off my texts—and I admit, I like a challenge, so I kept texting her back. But once she wanted to get serious, I was like, No way. I was only into the game." –JENS, 18

HIS BROS DON'T APPROVE.
"Once I ended things with a girl just because my friends didn't like her. The way I see it, girls come and go, but my friends will be here forever, so obviously their opinions matter to me." –FORD, 19

way harsh!

how to tell if you're in *love*

Your feelings about a guy can be tricky to define, so here's how to know if it's the real deal.

you're comfortable not wearing makeup around him.

When you don't stress about covering up a zit, it means you can let down your guard and show him the real you. You trust that he's not going to make fun of or judge you.

you feel your best with him.

Instead of worrying if he likes you or not, you'll know you are in love because being around your guy makes you feel more confident and sure of yourself in every way!

you like his imperfections.

Most relationships start with attraction, but being in love helps you recognize the quirky things that make a guy special. Even more important, you won't want to change them!

you're okay with fighting.

If you want to find a new guy after every argument, you're just crushing. When you're in love, you choose to work through your disagreements because you know how much you enjoy having him in your life.

you don't want to play games.

In the beginning, you may test him by flirting with other guys and checking to see if he gets jealous. When you're in love, he doesn't have to keep proving himself to you over and over.

GET TO KNOW...
JORDAN

AGE 19

RELATIONSHIP STATUS Single

CELEBRITY CRUSH Selena Gomez

THE BEST WAY TO DTR WITH A GUY "Talk to him in person—not through text! That way, you'll get a direct answer and a sense of how he's feeling throughout the conversation based on his body language."

WHAT I LOOK FOR IN A GIRLFRIEND "I want a smart girl who also likes to have fun (and likes to cuddle!)."

HOW I KNEW I WAS IN LOVE FOR THE FIRST TIME "I first knew I was in love after my ex and I split. Usually when a relationship ends, I feel hurt, but I know I'll be OK with time. But when my most recent ex and I broke up, it felt like I'd lost a major thing in my life. I finally told her I was in love with her, and after she took time to think about it, we got back together!"

is *he* in love with you?

Your guy might not have the guts to come out and say it, but there *are* signs that he's feeling it too!

HE USES THE "L" WORD.

When he starts to think his feelings for you are love, he'll use the actual word more often in conversation. ("I love hanging out with you.") He's testing out your reaction!

HE LOVES YOUR FRIENDS.

If your guy invites your friends to hang out or gives them advice about guy stuff, it's because he cares about you so much that everyone you love has become important to him by extension.

HE FINGER-LACES.

When he grabs your hand, does he intertwine his fingers with yours? That tight grip is his way of communicating how tight your bond is, too.

HE HAS ROUTINES.

Does your guy always have phone convos the same way (like by saying a special good-night phrase)? Those routines reinforce how important you are to him. If he didn't see a real future with you, he wouldn't make you such a regular part of his life!

HE REACHES OUT WHEN HE'S AWAY.

If he has major feelings for you, an "I miss you" text is his way of keeping your connection strong. That's because the closeness he feels with you boosts his hormone levels. When he is apart from you and doesn't get that same buzz, it legitimately bums him out—and he needs a fix.

"Being infatuated with someone, that's not really love. Love is a pretty special thing—it feels a lot better than just being obsessed."
–Liam Hemsworth

BOOST YOUR BOND!

If you're not *quite* trading "Love u, babe!" texts yet, these tricks will bring you closer!

ask crazy Qs!

Solid couples know each other better than anyone, but not necessarily through super-deep, forced convos. Ask zany questions like, "Whose life would you steal?" or play games of text Truth or Dare. You'll start to uncover each other's hopes and dreams—in a fun way.

team up!

Taking on a joint project gives you that amazing "Yay, we did it!" feeling—which is a completely different rush from a regular date night. Try painting your bedroom, volunteering, or making dinner for friends—anything where you're working together.

celebrate!

In-love couples don't just support each other in a passive "good luck" way—they're truly psyched to live in each other's big moments. So when he scores a big goal or gets into his dream school, be the first to head up the after-party. He'll know you're on his side.

"why i *fell* for her"

Get the inside scoop on what makes guys go nuts for you!

her passion!

"I love how driven my girlfriend is about ballet, from the way she cares for her shoes to her careful warm-up routine. That kind of focus and dedication is the same stuff that makes her an awesome girlfriend."

–Matthew, 21

her devotion!

"My girlfriend makes a point to come to all my track meets and brings cute, handmade posters. I feel good knowing that even when I don't have the best race, she's still my biggest fan."

–Erving, 17

her thoughtfulness!

"One Saturday morning, my girlfriend showed up at my house to surprise me with banana-chocolate-chip pancakes! The fact that she would plan something special for no reason made me feel special, too."

–Caleb, 20

how to say "*i love you*" (without freaking him out!)

If you're bursting at the seams to say these three magic words, here's how to make sure he's ready to hear them!

Q: **What does it take to get a guy to say "I love you"?**

A: "I had never really thought about being in love until one day, while my girlfriend and I were hanging out, I looked over at her and we were just smiling at each other for no apparent reason. In that moment, it hit me. I knew I loved her! I'm a fairly shy person, so I was nervous to tell her right then, but I did because I knew it was real and wanted her to know. And she told me she loved me, too. It was the best feeling in the world!"

–MICHAEL, 21

WHEN...

DO wait it out.
Love is an amazing feeling, but keep your feelings to yourself for a few weeks so you can sort them out. When you do say it, you'll know it's not just on a whim.

DON'T jump the gun.
Two months or less is too soon! That OMG-he's-perfect feeling you get early on in a relationship is just a taste of the heaping plates of love that come next.

WHERE...

DO say it after a date.
Tell him after a perfect evening together. Saying "I love you" is like taking a picture: You'll remember the moment forever, so capture something good!

DON'T say it after a fight.
Your first "I love you" should be a happy moment, not in the midst of a tearful apology (when you're not thinking straight) or because you want him to forgive you.

HOW...

DO kiss him!
Tell him how you feel, then plant one on him! The sweet gesture will give him a second to gather his thoughts—so he can get the guts to say it back!

DON'T give a long disclaimer.
Like, "You don't have to say anything back, but…" If you're not sure he's ready to say it, wait, so you don't pressure him to say something he doesn't feel.

score!

YOU'RE BOYFRIEND AND GIRLFRIEND!

Y ou've DTR-ed and changed your Facebook status to "in a relationship," and even though you've been dating for a while now, admit it: this is kind of the best. thing. ever. You've got a guy who adores you, so how do you make that super-happy-all-the-time feeling he gives you last forever? The ultimate relationship secrets here will do the trick!

be the *ultimate* girlfriend!

Real guys tell you how to go from ordinary to A+.

HOW TO:

support his hobby

AN AVERAGE GIRLFRIEND...
Cheers him on at the big game or show.

AN AWESOME GIRLFRIEND...
Cheers him on at the small game or show.

"Everyone in school comes when my band, Forty Winters, plays on Friday night. But when my girl drops by a practice or listens to me try new material, that matters more—like she really gets how important it is to me."

–Kevin, 20

HOW TO:

plan a Saturday night

AN AVERAGE GIRLFRIEND...
Asks him what he wants to do.

AN AWESOME GIRLFRIEND...
Surprises him!

"For Valentine's Day, my girl made me dinner and took me to a NASCAR race—it was a total surprise. Taking the time to plan something so different showed me how much she cares about us."

–Dominique, 19

HOW TO:

chill with his friends

AN AVERAGE GIRLFRIEND...
Has girls' nights when he has guys' nights.

AN AWESOME GIRLFRIEND...
Contributes to guys' night every once in a while.

"My ex would just sit around and watch me play video games with my friends. But my new girl understands our nerd game lingo and doesn't roll her eyes when we tell guy jokes. It's awesome!"

–Rick, 18

HOW TO:

do PDA the right way

AN AVERAGE GIRLFRIEND...
Avoids it (so he's not embarrassed).

AN AWESOME GIRLFRIEND...
Embraces it (so he feels like a stud!).

"One time a girlfriend grabbed me and kissed me in the library—which was hot! I like it when a girl is not afraid to show how much she digs me in front of everyone—it's actually very sexy and sweet!"

–Rob, 19

SNEAKY WAYS
to make him *worship* you

You know the girlfriend who's got her guy wrapped around her finger? With these tricks, it could be *you.*

1
greet him with a compliment.

When your guy knows he has your approval, he'll work to keep it. So take a second to look him over, then say, "That shirt is so hot on you!" Now he'll always dress to impress you…lucky girl!

2
suggest something.

Guys love a girl who brings fun to the table, so always have an idea ready—like trying that new sushi place. You'll avoid the "I don't know—what do you want to do?" trap (worship sabotage!) and be more likely to get your way.

3
remember the small stuff.

Want him hanging on your every word? Bringing up the details that he mentioned in past conversations is a surprisingly effective way to make your guy pay more attention to you in return!

4
call him on his crap.

If he does something jerky, calmly tell him why it bummed you out. When he feels responsible for making you sad, he'll try to make it right in the future (whereas blowing up will just make him defensive).

THE ULTIMATE SECRETS OF HAPPY COUPLES!

The winners of *Seventeen's* Best Couples in America contest share the secrets that will make you and your guy more in love than ever!

choose the *right* guy!

These guys all have a reason why they're Best Boyfriend winners! Choose the best type for *you:*

1
the supporter

"When my dad got cancer, Curtis kept me on track—making sure I went to class, helping me study, even bringing me my fave foods. Curtis says if you can't be with someone at their worst, you don't deserve to be with them at their best. It made me feel safe to know that I could always lean on him—like everything was going to be all right."

–his girlfriend, Lysandra

2
the best friend

"For our one-year anniversary, Kyle and I decided to make each other gifts instead of buying them. He made me two canvas paintings: One of him speaking into a tin can phone, the other of me listening with the words *I love you* coming out of the can. I couldn't help but cry when I saw them. He's just the most thoughtful person."

–his girlfriend, Katie

3
the fighter

"Even though my family disapproved of him because of cultural differences—Paul is Korean, and I'm Fillipino-Chinese—he just wouldn't give up trying to win them over. Instead of acting angry, he stayed respectful by making a point of hanging out with my family and getting to know them too."

–his girlfriend, Rachelle

4
the fun one

"James and I have been dating for almost three years—but he never lets things get boring. He will pick me up and take me to an amusement park—just because! James doesn't save all the attention for a special occasion—he does those sweet little things every single day."

–his girlfriend, Meghan

5
the nice guy

"What I love most about Zac is his forgiveness. Like if we have a fight, he'll say, 'Let's sit here, listen to each other, and work this out.' And we always do. He's shown me that it pays to go for the nice guy—and stop wasting my time with bad-asses!"

–his girlfriend, Janelle

IS YOUR GUY BEST BOYFRIEND MATERIAL?

The Best BFs explain the sneaky ways to tell if your crush is a keeper.

HE DOESN'T HIDE ANYTHING!

"When my ex kept texting me, I told my GF, Mimi, about it instead of hiding it from her. Then I changed my number so my ex couldn't reach me, because I wanted to show Mimi that no one would ever come between us!"

—CHRIS

HE SHARES YOUR BELIEFS!

"You have to be on the same page and make sure you both have the same morals. Madie and I are both really spiritual, and we met through a friend at a church event. Because we have the same faith, we can really open up to each other and talk about anything."

—RYAN

HE TREATS OTHERS WELL!

"If a guy isn't nice to everyone, from his friends to strangers— even his mom—he's just putting on a front when he's nice to you. Katie likes that I take other people's feelings into account."

—KYLE

don't fall for a *bad* bf...

Need advice re: your relationship? Ask yourself, What Would the Best BFs Do?

Q My BF of more than a year still hangs out with his friends way more than he does with me! What do I do?

A "Say something like, 'It really bothers me that you're always at your friends' house.' If he really cares, he'll make an effort to change things because he'll want you to feel important."

–Curtis

Q My BF is going away to college, but I'm still a junior. I'm afraid he's going to meet another girl. Help!

A "Try not to worry about what might happen—focus on having fun with him now. Jess and I are going to school two hours apart, so I try to just enjoy the time we have together."

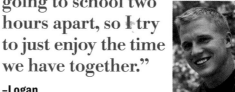

–Logan

Q I want to surprise my boyfriend by doing something really sweet that he'd never suspect. Any ideas?

A "Pay attention to the things your guy likes. Hannah surprised me for our two-year anniversary with a picnic. She brought tuna salad sandwiches—my favorite! It was really thoughtful."

–Lane

WARNING!

Not every dude is award-winning material. These Best BFs tell you how to spot the losers.

HE DOESN'T APOLOGIZE.

"One guy I know left his girlfriend out of the loop when he was making plans for the weekend, and she got upset. Instead of admitting that it was wrong, he just pretended like he'd never seen her text asking to hang out. A real man never has too much pride to say that he's sorry."

–Dakota

HE WON'T COMMIT.

"When I was on the football team, guys would talk about seeing three girls at one time. They got away with it because they'd tell girls they didn't want to be official. That's what guys say when they want a 'get out of jail free' card for cheating."

–Jorge

HE WANTS AN INSTANT HOOKUP.

"All of my guy friends have told me they want to be in relationships, but they also go to parties and have random hookups. So if you meet someone you like, don't hook up with him right away. That tells him that you're looking for something more serious than one night of fun."

–Thomas

create a super-glue tight *bond!*

These winning couples share how to get closer than ever!

LOOK AT HIS SIDE OF THINGS.

"If I didn't look at things from her perspective, I would never be able to truly understand what she's feeling."

–JAKE

OPEN UP TO EACH OTHER.

"Jake and I had been dating for five months, and I felt like our relationship had hit a dead end. Jake and I had a long talk, where I said he needed to be more open with his feelings or else we were breaking up. Jake did a complete turnaround and told me all the time how much he cared about me. He stopped being afraid to put his emotions out there, which made me realize that I really loved him."

–HIS GIRLFRIEND, ABBY

BE A SHOULDER TO LEAN ON.

"I do anything I can to support Kate because she supports me too. No one in my family ever talked to me about college, but Kate took me to look at schools, fill out my applications, and register for classes. She is always there for me, helping me get through it all. The least I can do is return the favor."

–JORGE

HAVE SECRETS.

"When we can tell the other person is having a bad day, we leave a note in their car. And Jorge has this secret hand signal when we're together: Two squeezes mean: 'I love you.' It's his way of reminding me that he's right there beside me if I'm ever starting to freak out about something!"

–HIS GIRLFRIEND, KATE

DON'T JUDGE EACH OTHER.

"Great communication goes both ways. You can be honest, but the other person has to really listen. I know I can tell Allison anything and she won't judge me—even when I do something I'm not proud of, like blowing a test. She's helped me let my guard down—and that's what made us grow so close."

–DAKOTA

BE HONEST!

"A few weeks ago, Dakota and I had this stupid fight at a party. On the way home, we talked about it, and soon we were both crying—in a good way. We knew we could be totally honest with each other."

–HIS GIRLFRIEND, ALLISON

BE YOURSELF.

"One night, after a Halloween party at my school, we just talked. Everyone else had left early to party, but Karen said straight up, 'I don't drink.' She doesn't care what anyone else thinks is cool—she is totally her own person. From the first moment I met her, that was so interesting to me."

–THOMAS

LAUGH A LITTLE!

"I used to be a tough cookie to crack—kind of shy and serious. But Thomas's crazy humor cut right through that."

–HIS GIRLFRIEND, KAREN

SHOW YOUR DEDICATION.

"When she wants to learn something, she'll spend hours studying or performing it. If she can be that dedicated, then so can I."

–BRANDON

DO SWEET THINGS FOR EACH OTHER!

"The sweetest thing Brandon has ever done for me was the video he made to ask me to prom—it took him sixty hours! It showed him packing up and traveling to my house in California, and at the end, he told me to go outside. There he was on my doorstep with roses!"

–HIS GIRLFRIEND, GABRIELLE

his *mushiest* love confessions!

These hotties might seem tough—but it turns out they're total softies. Is your guy hiding a sweet side?

"I saved the first text message my girlfriend ever sent to me, and I read it all the time. It said she was at a party thinking about me. It's the first time I realized something could happen between us."

–Hans, 20

"My ex girlfriend basically forced me to watch *The Notebook*. I tried so hard to hate it, but by the end I couldn't hold back anymore. I was bawling my eyes out!"

–Philip, 19

"I'm a really big sap for my three sisters, especially my twin. When I talk about them, I get very emotional because they mean so much to me. I don't think that I could be the man I am today if I didn't have them in my life."

–Chris, 21

"I have two miniature dachshunds, and when I come home from college, I can't wait to snuggle with them!"

–Dan, 19

"When my girlfriend gets upset, and starts to cry, I've been known to start crying too—I just hate seeing her so sad!"

–Garret, 18

"I keep all the love letters my girlfriend ever wrote me in a shoe box in my closet. She's my first love, so I want to remember everything!"

–Derek, 20

WHAT HE THINKS ABOUT...
you and *other guys!*

When you're official, where does he draw the line between being friendly with other dudes ... and a foul play?

being close with your ex

TOTALLY FINE "I think it's a good thing when a girl that you're dating can be friendly with her ex-boyfriend. It shows that she's a mature person!"
—SHAMIR, 19

CROSSING THE LINE "If he's saved in your phone with a pet name like Such a Hottie, that would make me feel like I didn't measure up— and that you're not over him!"
—ANDREW, 19

texting your guy's friends

TOTALLY FINE "I wouldn't be bothered as long as she was friends with my friend before we started dating. New relationships shouldn't mess up old friendships."
—ETHAN, 17

CROSSING THE LINE "If she hides the text from me, I'd definitely think they were doing something behind my back!"
—NICK, 16

flirting at a party

TOTALLY FINE "I wouldn't be too upset if my girl was making small talk with other guys, or laughing at their jokes. She's just being social!"
—JEFFREY, 21

CROSSING THE LINE "Once she starts acting clingy and hanging all over a guy, I'd either tell her she's not worth my time or leave her at the party. That's embarrassing!"
—ADAM, 19

hanging with his bros

TOTALLY FINE "I'd like it if my girlfriend hung out with my guy friends, unless they started liking her more than me! Then I would become jealous of her!"
—NICHOLAS, 17

CROSSING THE LINE "Spending time with my friends is okay, but don't start comparing me to them. I don't want to know if you think my friend is cuter than me!"
—JOSHUA, 18

SNEAKY WAYS
to make
long distance work!

It's you versus the 500 miles between you and your BF.
But with these tricks, you'll feel closer than ever!

1
schedule skype dates!

When you're just a voice on the phone, it can make you feel disconnected. Give him a mental picture of your life: Show off your dorm décor and introduce him to your roomies. It's as close as he can get to being there.

2
make mornings matter!

You're both so immersed in separate worlds that it's hard to find the time to catch up. Stay on his mind all day with a flirty text, like, "Hey, sleepyhead. Woke up thinking abt u! <3" It's a quick way to keep your connection strong.

3
plan each visit as if it's NBD.

When face-time is sparse, there's pressure to make each trip feel like a holiday and overplan. Stick to things you'd normally do together, like ordering pizza. A low-key vibe will help you both feel the way you did before you had to take two trains and a bus to see each other.

4
experience things together!

Plan to see TV shows like *The X Factor* on Hulu before bed and text each other what you think as you're watching. It's something to look forward to when you're bored thinking about him in class, and in the moment, it will feel as if you're sitting right next to him!

ARE YOU PLANNING A SURPRISE VISIT?

DO IT THIS WAY...

"My girlfriend and I met in college, but she graduated a year early and moved hours away to job hunt. When she landed a job back in our college town, she planned a surprise trip to tell me in person! It was so much better than hearing the news over the phone because we got to celebrate together."
–SALEEM, 21

...NOT THIS WAY!

"One morning, I rolled over in bed in my college dorm and my girlfriend from home was just lying there. I asked her what she was doing, and she said she wanted to surprise me. I was super creeped out! Knock on his door instead!"
–AUSTIN, 19

UGH, SO YOU
broke up...

Fact: Breakups suck. Suddenly the person who made you jump out of bed at just the thought of seeing him is out of your life...and all you can think about is *why*. Read on, because this advice is exactly what you need to pick up the pieces, so that in your next relationship, you're stronger and smarter than ever!

"why i broke up with you"

All you want is the truth, and he's finally got an honest answer.
Here's the closure every girl needs!

"You were way too clingy!"

Dear S,

When I first met you, I thought you had the world's greatest personality.

Little did I know that, after just a month and a half of dating, you'd become the "Queen of Cling." There were the constant phone calls—seven of them in a row at 1 a.m., just to talk. And if I was tagged in a photo with other girls on Facebook, you'd message them, asking why they were in a picture with me. I never said so while we were dating, but all of this really freaked me out, and I broke up with you because I needed to get my independence back!

–Cody, 18

"Your parents wouldn't let us be together."

Dear A,

Every time I see you wearing those gold-feathered earrings, I think of that one night when we were walking around after dinner, and under the trees, we kissed in the rain. I know every day could have been like that if your parents had only let us be together.

We were young—both of us were just fifteen, after all—and I get that your mom wanted you to focus on school, but I couldn't believe how controlling she was. I tried to deal with our relationship being secret for seven months, but eventually, it got pretty hard only being able to see you in school. My feelings for you started to go away, and my friends kept telling me it wasn't worth it to stay with you, so I ended it.

I hope the next guy can wait a little longer, until your parents will let you date—I couldn't wait long enough. And when he does come along, I hope you'll be able to speak up about what you want.

–Jose, 17

"I was just using you."

Dear L,

When we met, my first serious relationship had just ended. I was heartbroken! And when you started flirting with me, I hadn't felt wanted like that in a long time. I completely let my hormones take over and jumped at the first girl I saw—which was you. After two months of hooking up, when you asked where our relationship was going—a perfectly understandable question after that long—I felt like a total jerk. It forced me to realize that I wasn't being honest with myself about why I was hooking up with someone so casually. Basically, I was using you to get over my ex-girlfriend. I know this makes me sound like a bad person, but now I understand that, to me, our relationship was a "rebound." I had a busted ego, and hooking up with you made me feel better about myself.

–Robb, 20

"I was cheating on you."

Dear B,

I finally want to be honest with you about why we broke up. When we met at summer camp, you knew I had just split up with my ex-girl-friend, M. The truth is, after we came home, I was hooking up with you and M for about a month.

You and M went to different schools, so I thought I could get away with dating both of you while I figured out my feelings. When you eventually asked if I was seeing someone else, I lied and said no. Our relationship was brand-new and I didn't want to risk losing you yet, so I dumped M to be with you.

Then one night, I was driving you home, and I got a text from M saying, "I love you still." All of the good memories with M came rushing back, and we had such a history together. I decided to give her one last shot, and that's when I broke up with you.

Of course, M and I didn't last. I know what I did was awful, and to this day it's the biggest regret of my life. I was young and selfish, and I didn't know the right way to sort through my feelings. It's been two years since we've spoken, but I still love you, B. If I could take it back and do it all over again, I would do anything to be with you.

–Josh, 20

"Getting your heart broken is something everyone has to go through. (My family and my friends were extremely important to talk to.) I think the only way to get through it is just talk about it as soon as it happens, but then, it's really important to move on and forget about it—because there comes a point where the more you talk about it, the more it's just going to hurt you."
–Taylor Lautner

why guys *dump* girls they still like

The real reason might have nothing to do with you!

HIS REASON

he doesn't have time.

"During my first year of college, I dated a girl while pledging a fraternity. I got so into hanging out with my new brothers that she just didn't fit in anymore. I liked her, but I wanted to party and do the frat-guy thing more."
—MICHAEL, 20

HIS REASON

he's shy.

"I really liked this girl I was seeing, but things were at a standstill because I was too stinking shy to tell her how I felt, and she didn't say anything either. Neither of us was willing to move things forward, so I just ended it. I wish I'd had more guts."
—MATT, 21

HIS REASON

JERK ALERT!

he's using you.

"One time I dated a girl as a stepping stone to dating her best friend. She was great—but her friend was better!"
—ADAM, 20

HIS REASON

he's broke.

"Girlfriends are expensive, especially if you don't have a job. I dated a girl I really liked, but I was too embarrassed to tell her that I couldn't afford going out to dinner and movies all the time, so I just called things off."
—JERRY, 17

HIS REASON

he didn't want to be apart.

"I had a girlfriend who was getting ready to leave for a year-long study abroad program in France. I hated the idea of being apart from her, so I dealt with it by picking fights all the time. Eventually I made her so miserable that she broke up with me."
—BRIAN, 18

"Everyone [makes mistakes in love], and you only learn from it. Mistakes build character! My greatest lesson is find yourself before you find another person."
–Chris Zylka

Q: I'll admit it: I cheated in our relationship, but he won't admit how he really feels about it. What's he going through?

A: "When it happened to me, I turned to my closest guy friends for advice. They told me to move on and meet a bunch of other girls—but not to hook up with anyone until I really thought it through. I'd been really down on myself, but spending time with my friends finally made me snap out of it. I could forget how hurt I was and have fun instead."
—PAUL, 21

what i *never* told my ex

These guys are finally getting a few secrets off their chest.

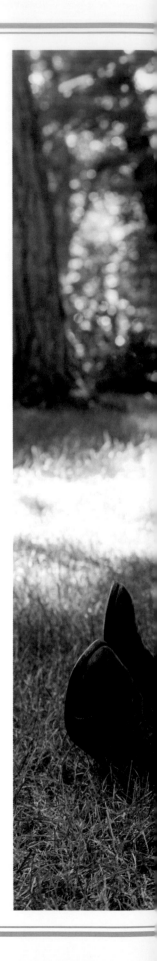

I DESPISED YOUR SHOES!

"I never told my ex-girlfriend how much I disliked her Uggs. They were completely hideous!"

–Erick, 18

....

I HATED HOW YOU SPOKE!

"My ex never knew how annoying I thought it was that she used the word 'like' in every sentence!"

–Drew, 21

....

I LIKED YOUR FRIEND!

"My ex didn't know I had a crush on her friend–but she should have…I was always inviting her along!"

–Adam, 17

....

I COULDN'T STAND YOUR BREATH!

"I never let her know how bad her breath smelled! It would totally kill the mood when we'd make out, so I started offering her breath mints and popping one myself–just so it wasn't too obvious."

–Ryan, 18

....

 ### I STILL LOVE YOU!

"I never told her how much I miss her. My friends told me not to say anything–that it was so much better being single. But I really would like to be with her again."

–Lorenzo, 15

your 5-step recovery plan

Your BFFs are already on their way over with ice cream in hand. Here are other important ways to help yourself heal!

1
MOPE

Go ahead, put on comfy sweats, then make this promise to yourself: "I'm going to give myself five days to watch crappy movies, eat ice cream, and feel heartbroken. Then I'm going to start feeling better." Telling yourself that you'll get through this gives you control of your feelings, not him.

2
IGNORE HIM

Talking to him might seem helpful (I just want to hear his voice!), but it only re-opens the wound. So delete his number, de-friend him on Facebook, and take the hallway route that doesn't pass his locker. (You can try to be friends later, after you've moved on.)

3
CLEAN UP

Get rid of anything that reminds you of him. If you can't bear to trash it for good, give it to a friend, so you don't have to see it on a daily basis. (She can give it back to you when you both agree you're over him.) If you have stuff he needs back, ask her to return it for you.

4
STAY BUSY

Pinpoint the times you miss him the most (do you still listen for that last text before you fall asleep?), and fill them with something else: Re-read *Beautiful Creatures*, listen to One Direction, whatever. If you keep yourself distracted, the sadness will eventually fade on its own.

5
FLIRT!

While you don't want to jump into anything while you're still getting over your ex, flirting with new guys is a great way to keep your mind off your heartache. Start by asking a cute guy friend to take you to dinner. Even a non-date will remind you that there are good guys out there!

have a *happy* breakup!

Take it from readers who've been there—you *can* move on without all the messiness.

take the high road.

"I was so hurt when my BF broke up with me out of the blue, but I promised myself that I wouldn't bash him— even when my friends called him a jerk. I didn't want to linger over the pain. Letting go helped me move on."

–JULIA, 17

go Facebook MIA.

"After I broke up with my boyfriend, I knew I'd get flooded with FB comments as soon as I changed my status to 'single'—so I didn't go on for a week. When I finally did, I posted only happy stuff so the drama would die down."

–JESSICA, 16

keep the deets quiet.

"I shared the details of my breakup with just one person—my best friend. Refusing to talk about it to the whole world made it less likely to turn into gossip that would come back to haunt me."

–JEN, 17

seventeen
HOT GUY
PANEL

GET TO KNOW...
JASON

AGE 18

RELATIONSHIP STATUS Single

CELEBRITY CRUSH Ariana Grande

THE BEST WAY TO DTR WITH A GUY "Be straight up with him! It's OK to ask him what his intentions are—you don't want to waste your time on someone who doesn't feel the same way you do."

WHAT I LOOK FOR IN A GIRLFRIEND "I love when she takes charge and plans the date sometimes. Girls aren't the only ones who like a surprise!"

HOW I KNEW I WAS IN LOVE FOR THE FIRST TIME "I caught myself thinking about her all the time. When I was ready to tell her how I felt, I had butterflies in my stomach, but when I looked into her eyes, I felt so comfortable. I said it and she said it back … it was a perfect moment!"

is he a player?

He could be a huge flirt, or a massive fake.
Take this quiz and find out for sure.

START HERE AND CHECK THE STATEMENTS
THAT SOUND LIKE HIM.

☐ He loves to hug you hello.

☐ He loves to hug every girl hello.

☐ He writes the sweetest compliments to you
via text or through a private DM on Twitter
(but no public posts yet).

☐ Once he uncovers something quirky about you, like
your obsession with red Starbursts, he remembers it.

☐ You find something to laugh about almost
every time you're together.

☐ He'll go MIA for weeks, but when you hear
from him again, he's very apologetic.

☐ He regularly posts funny YouTube videos
on your Facebook timeline.

☐ When you go to parties together, it sometimes feels
like you're fighting for one-on-one time with him.

☐ He's a last-minute planner and usually waits
until the day of to ask if you're free.

☐ When there's major drama at home,
he wants to talk to you about it.

☐ He's super-fun when he asks you out, but
he's rarely available when you ask him out.

☐ When you text, there's a ton of flirty
back-and-forth but less day-to-day stuff.

MOSTLY BLUE

he's a romantic!

You have nothing to worry about—this guy is into you!
Check the good-guy signs: posts on your timeline,
deep personal talks, or a giant bag of your favorite
candy just because. Don't overly second-guess his
sweetness or he'll feel you don't trust him.

MOSTLY GREEN

he's a flirt!

Your crush isn't shady; he's just outgoing! The next
move is up to you. If you want to keep things casual,
you can't freak out every time another girl is at
his locker. But to take things to the next level, he'll
need a direct approach. Try something light, like,
"You and me…on a real date. Thoughts?"

MOSTLY AQUA

he's a player!

This guy knows all the right things to say so that
you—and every other girl—will be totally into him.
Still think you're in his inner circle? Is he gushy in
private but sort of cold in public? Does he heap on
the attention and then disappear for two weeks?
Don't play his game. Cut him loose ASAP.

what do *guys love* about you?

When you know what dudes are dialed into, you can use it to your advantage!

START HERE

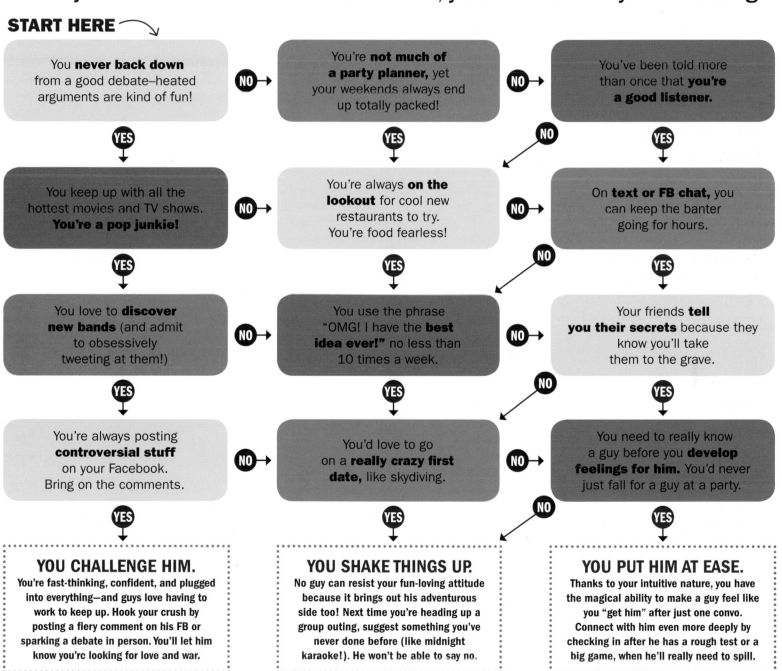

You **never back down** from a good debate—heated arguments are kind of fun!

NO → You're **not much of a party planner,** yet your weekends always end up totally packed!

NO → You've been told more than once that **you're a good listener.**

YES ↓

You keep up with all the hottest movies and TV shows. **You're a pop junkie!**

NO → You're always **on the lookout** for cool new restaurants to try. You're food fearless!

NO → On **text or FB chat,** you can keep the banter going for hours.

YES ↓

You love to **discover new bands** (and admit to obsessively tweeting at them!)

NO → You use the phrase "OMG! I have the **best idea ever!**" no less than 10 times a week.

NO → Your friends **tell you their secrets** because they know you'll take them to the grave.

YES ↓

You're always posting **controversial stuff** on your Facebook. Bring on the comments.

NO → You'd love to go on a **really crazy first date,** like skydiving.

NO → You need to really know a guy before you **develop feelings for him.** You'd never just fall for a guy at a party.

YES ↓

YOU CHALLENGE HIM.
You're fast-thinking, confident, and plugged into everything—and guys love having to work to keep up. Hook your crush by posting a fiery comment on his FB or sparking a debate in person. You'll let him know you're looking for love and war.

YOU SHAKE THINGS UP.
No guy can resist your fun-loving attitude because it brings out his adventurous side too! Next time you're heading up a group outing, suggest something you've never done before (like midnight karaoke!). He won't be able to say no.

YOU PUT HIM AT EASE.
Thanks to your intuitive nature, you have the magical ability to make a guy feel like you "get him" after just one convo. Connect with him even more deeply by checking in after he has a rough test or a big game, when he'll really need to spill.

would your guy friend make a good *boyfriend?*

Admit it, the idea has crossed your mind. But is he *really* BF material? Check the signs that sound like him to find out.

☐ *he's tight with your friends.*

It might seem great to share the same crew–no awkward introduction or choosing who to hang out with. But in a relationship, **you'd have zero privacy,** and it might be impossible to make love decisions without everyone's input. Plus, a breakup could break up your whole group.

☐ *he flakes.*

Friendship doesn't have a lot of rules, so it's no big deal if **he forgets to text** when he said he would, or if he peaces out at a party without saying good-bye. But if he's truly unreliable, he won't magically become Mr. Dependable just because you're dating.

☐ *he's your "fun" friend.*

He cracks you up and makes every night out more fun. But if you've tried to talk to him when you're freaking out about college apps or fighting with your parents and he doesn't want to engage in **those personal convos,** he might be better off as a surface-level friend.

MOSTLY THIS COLUMN

NO! You guys know each other pretty well and have fun together, but it's not likely that things will go deeper. (One clue: it hasn't already, so you guys didn't have that initial spark.) It's not like you could never date, but it would require **starting from scratch**–you'd have to get to know each other in a new light.

☐ *he's not too touchy-feely.*

Your buddy hugs you hello, drapes his arm around you, or sometimes tries to tickle you until you scream. When the touchiness stops there–like **he doesn't try to get you alone at parties** or push you to make out–it says that he cares about you as a person, not as a hookup.

☐ *you share a language.*

When you read his texts, can you practically hear his voice in your head? And when you're talking, does he usually get what you're trying to say before you even finish your sentence? When you **just get each other like that,** it means you could connect on a deeper level.

☐ *he's honest with you.*

You know when you ask his opinion he'll tell you your new sunglasses are "kinda weird," or that your latest crush isn't interested. **A guy who's not afraid to tell you the truth** won't be fake to try to get you to like him–his straight talk is a sign he respects you.

MOSTLY THIS COLUMN

YES! Your friendship already has **the traits that make a relationship great**–so taking it to the next level could bring you amazing love. If you want to take that step, ask him if he wants to have a night out, just the two of you. It will give you a chance to feel out your chemistry–and if it's not there, just call your other friends to join you.

is he *feeling it* or faking it?

Some guys act super-lovey, then disappear. Find out if your fling will last.

CHECK THE STATEMENTS THAT APPLY

Christopher French & Ashley Tisdale

Matt Prokop & Sarah Hyland

☐ He holds your **hand.**

☐ He holds your **hand (and your bags).**

Josh Bowman & Emily VanCamp

☐ He looks at you **lovingly.**

☐ He looks at you **crazily.**

Ashton Kutcher & Mila Kunis

☐ He walks **in front of you.**

☐ He walks **next to you.**

Naya Rivera & Big Sean

☐ He gets **close to you** in photos.

☐ He **sends** you pics of himself.

Annalynne McCord & Dominic Purcell

☐ He's obsessed with his **car.**

☐ He's up for a **stroll.**

Selena Gomez & Austin Butler

Louis Tomlinson & Eleanor Calder

Andrew Garfield & Emma Stone

Bella Thorne & Tristan Klier

MOSTLY ORANGE

he's feeling it!

Love is in the details, and a guy who finds small ways to be romantic (hauling your stuff!) or remembers your conversations from three weeks ago isn't just looking for a random hookup–he's zeroed in on you. You're on the road to a relationship. Enjoy it!

MOSTLY PINK

he's faking it!

A guy who comes on strong fizzles out fast. Sure, his fancy dates and mushy texts catch your attention, but is he paying attention to *you*? If his moves seem weirdly impersonal, like he's pulling them out of some "Hookup Handbook," he's not looking for a relationship.

is your *love history* holding you back?

You think your ex is old news—but he could still be screwing up your love life.

START HERE

☐ You still text your ex but not constantly like before—more like once a week.

☐ You know which friends keep in touch with your ex, and you can't help hitting them up for info sometimes.

☐ Every time you flirt with someone new, you automatically compare him to your last BF.

☐ When you see your ex flirting with another girl at a party, you get a little pang of jealousy—but you'd never tell anyone.

☐ When you realize you have a reason to text your ex (like your missing hoodie must be at his place), you're secretly excited.

☐ You're convinced that all guys break hearts, lie, cheat, etc.

☐ You've told your ex that it's okay for you guys to talk about other people you're dating, now that you're on friendly terms.

☐ If you know you'll see your ex, you think through what you'll say, just to make sure you get it right.

☐ You wish you could just hurry up and get to college. A change in scenery is the only way you'll truly get over your relationship.

☐ You still have all your old text and chat conversations with your ex, but you haven't even thought about looking at them in ages.

☐ Every time you go to a place where your ex hangs out, you feel hyper-aware of the possibility of running into him.

☐ You've openly dissed your ex. People deserve to know what he was really like.

MOSTLY BLUE

move on!

You may have broken up, but your ex is still a major presence in your life. You don't have to stay so friendly—giving yourself a fresh start is not only okay but also smart and gutsy.

MOSTLY GREEN

cut him off!

Finding reasons to talk (and hook up) with your ex drags out breakup pain. For every setback, do one thing to move forward (i.e., texting someone new). Take it one step at a time.

MOSTLY AQUA

chill out!

You're so blinded by heartache, you wouldn't see a new hottie right in front of you! Channel your anger into something positive: Write songs, launch a blog. It's a fast way to move on.

are you a good *flirt?*

Let's see if you need to step up your game.

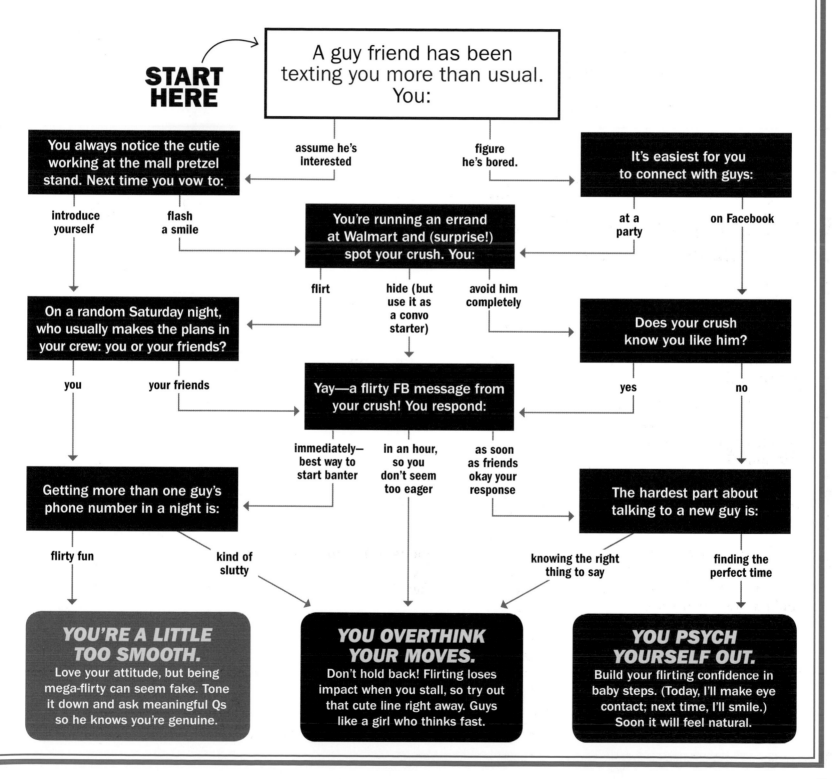

START HERE

A guy friend has been texting you more than usual. You:

assume he's interested

figure he's bored.

It's easiest for you to connect with guys:

You always notice the cutie working at the mall pretzel stand. Next time you vow to:

introduce yourself

flash a smile

You're running an errand at Walmart and (surprise!) spot your crush. You:

at a party

on Facebook

flirt

hide (but use it as a convo starter)

avoid him completely

Does your crush know you like him?

On a random Saturday night, who usually makes the plans in your crew: you or your friends?

you

your friends

Yay—a flirty FB message from your crush! You respond:

immediately— best way to start banter

in an hour, so you don't seem too eager

as soon as friends okay your response

yes

no

Getting more than one guy's phone number in a night is:

The hardest part about talking to a new guy is:

flirty fun

kind of slutty

knowing the right thing to say

finding the perfect time

YOU'RE A LITTLE TOO SMOOTH.
Love your attitude, but being mega-flirty can seem fake. Tone it down and ask meaningful Qs so he knows you're genuine.

YOU OVERTHINK YOUR MOVES.
Don't hold back! Flirting loses impact when you stall, so try out that cute line right away. Guys like a girl who thinks fast.

YOU PSYCH YOURSELF OUT.
Build your flirting confidence in baby steps. (Today, I'll make eye contact; next time, I'll smile.) Soon it will feel natural.

what makes you so *irresistible?*

You've got a secret sauce that guys go crazy for. Find it, then use it!

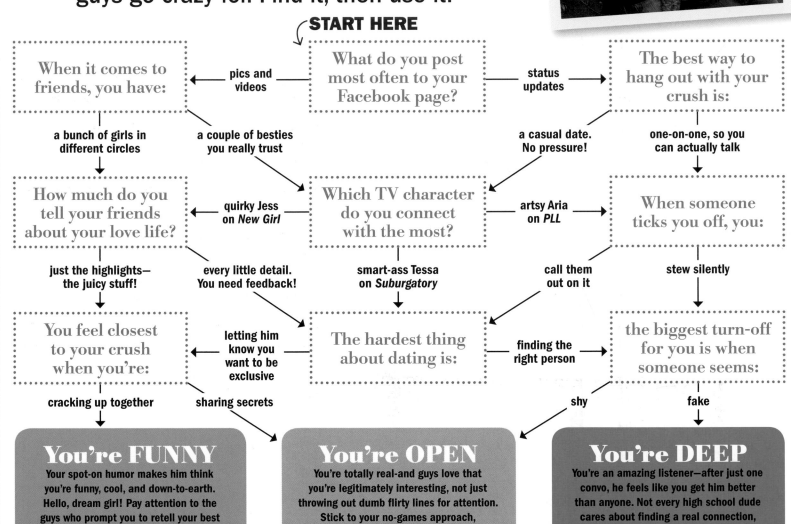

START HERE

When it comes to friends, you have:	← pics and videos — **What do you post most often to your Facebook page?** — status updates →	**The best way to hang out with your crush is:**

a bunch of girls in different circles

a couple of besties you really trust

a casual date. No pressure!

one-on-one, so you can actually talk

How much do you tell your friends about your love life?	← quirky Jess on *New Girl* — **Which TV character do you connect with the most?** — artsy Aria on *PLL* →	**When someone ticks you off, you:**

just the highlights— the juicy stuff!

every little detail. You need feedback!

smart-ass Tessa on *Suburgatory*

call them out on it

stew silently

You feel closest to your crush when you're:	← letting him know you want to be exclusive — **The hardest thing about dating is:** — finding the right person →	**the biggest turn-off for you is when someone seems:**

cracking up together

sharing secrets

shy

fake

You're FUNNY
Your spot-on humor makes him think you're funny, cool, and down-to-earth. Hello, dream girl! Pay attention to the guys who prompt you to retell your best stories or jokes—they're especially hypnotized by your awesomeness. Score!

You're OPEN
You're totally real-and guys love that you're legitimately interesting, not just throwing out dumb flirty lines for attention. Stick to your no-games approach, and soon you'll find a guy who's just as authentic as you are.

You're DEEP
You're an amazing listener—after just one convo, he feels like you get him better than anyone. Not every high school dude cares about finding a real connection, but once you weed through the duds, you'll find someone on your level.

are your *texts* :) or :(?

Are you sending your crush the wrong message—literally?!?

START HERE and check the statements that sound like you.

☐ You respond to texts **automatically**—dashing off "lmfao!" without thinking twice about it.

☐ When you're texting someone you like, you **play it cool**—no overdosing on the exclamation points.

☐ You're constantly adding a **flirty wink** to your messages. You need it to make your point! ;)

☐ Whenever you have that awkward moment when you're **not sure what a text means,** you just write back, "Ha!"

☐ One of your **flirtexting tricks** is to disappear mid-convo to leave the other person wanting more.

☐ You're not textclusive. You're always **talking to multiple hotties** at one time!

☐ You've thought about "accidentally" sending your crush a **text for someone else,** just to break the ice.

☐ Sometimes you show texts to friends to **get input** on what your crush really means, or how you should respond.

☐ You love to send **picture texts** to your crush when you see something funny.

☐ The best way to get to know a person is by playing text games, **like 20 questions.**

☐ When you **trade numbers** with cuties you're into, you definitely wait for them to text you first.

☐ If someone **stopped texting** you suddenly, it doesn't bug you—you make a point not to read into that stuff.

MOSTLY PINK
you're not connecting!

MOSTLY ORANGE
you're overthinking it!

You think carefully about getting every text exactly right—but obsessing too much about what you say makes the whole thing feel fake. Next time your crush sends you a message, type out the first thing that pops into your head (no filter!) and hit send. Flirting is more fun when you don't hold back!

MOSTLY RED
you're a textpert!

do you speak *dude?*

The Hot Guy Panel has a flirty line for you! How well do *you* read between the lines?

1 **ISMAEL SAYS** "What are you doing this weekend?"

HE MEANS
A Keep me posted on your plans
B I want to make sure I see you
C I'm free if nothing better comes up

2 **ELISEO SAYS** "Will your friend Lauren be there?"

HE MEANS
A I'm seriously into Lauren
B I don't want to hang out with just you
C Just wondering

3 **TREVOR SAYS** "'Nice pic' to your Facebook profile shot."

HE MEANS
A Just saying hi
B I'm secretly attracted to you
C I hope you message me

4 **JARED SAYS** "We should hang out sometime."

HE MEANS
A He'll text you soon
B Now the ball is in your court
C Let me know when you're free

5 **MICHAEL SAYS** "Can I have your number?"

HE MEANS
A You're fun to talk to
B I'll call you later
C I love knowing I can get your number

the results

1 ANSWER: C
"Unless I lock in exact plans with you, I'm just feeling out what's going on. You shouldn't expect to hear from me."
–Ismael, 19

2 ANSWER: A
"I admit: If I'm making a point to ask if a certain friend will be hanging out with us, I probably have a crush on her."
–Eliseo, 17

3 ANSWER: A
"I know it sounds like a compliment, but guys throw FB comments around pretty casually. Don't read into it too much."
–Trevor, 19

4 ANSWER: B
"A guy mentions hanging out as a test to see if you're interested. If you are, he expects that you'll make the next move."
–Jared, 17

5 ANSWER: C
"We get an ego boost from knowing we can score your number. It in no way means we actually plan to call. Sorry!"
–Michael, 20

3 OR LESS CORRECT **You're still learning the language.** You assume that what a guy says, he means. Flirting is all about subtle hints, so taking him literally gives you only half the story. Focus on his actions for real clues he likes you.

4 OR MORE CORRECT **You've mastered the lingo!** You know not to take what a guy says at face value— and because you're an expert at decoding lines, you'll always know exactly the right thing to say back. Keep it up, flirty girl!

are you addicted to *drama?*

When your love life gets messy, is a guy to blame—or are you?

START HERE and check the statements that sound like you.

☐ You like talking to several guys at once—one who is fun for parties, one who's up for long chats, one who's always available to give you a ride home, etc.

☐ It takes you a while to warm up to new guys—you **feel most comfortable** around the dudes you've known forever.

☐ You prefer to date guys **outside of your social circle**—you're done with all the guys from school!

☐ You don't mind if people at school talk about your relationship past or who you've hooked up with—it's flattering to know they're interested in you.

☐ If your crush found out **how often you check his Facebook profile,** you'd be beyond embarrassed!

☐ You're the first to admit that you don't always have the **best taste in guys**—but bad boys are so sexy!

☐ It's so weird, but somehow you always wind up at the party where a fight breaks out or something crazy happens. (And let's be honest, it's exciting!)

☐ You don't mind listening to your friends' gossip, but **you rarely tell your own stories**—you like to keep your stuff private!

☐ Confidence is a major turn-on for you. For example, you love when a guy **walks right up to you at a party** and starts laying on game.

☐ You have no problem meeting new guys, but it's frustrating how things always seem to fall apart or get messy before they become serious.

☐ Those guys at parties who seem like they're trying to show off on the dance floor or **hit on every girl in the room** seem totally fake to you.

☐ You know that **lots of other girls like your crush,** so it makes you feel extra-special when he calls you.

MOSTLY ORANGE
you love to stir up drama!
Guys are drawn to your outgoing life-of-the-party personality. But you'll do anything to keep from getting bored—like pick a fight with your crush just to create fireworks. It seems fun at first, but when you make a guy jump through hoops to be with you, he'll get tired of it fast.

MOSTLY PINK
you need more drama!

MOSTLY RED
you go for drama guys!

Photo Credits

OPENING SHOT
Terry Doyle

TOC
Chris Eckert/Studio D

HIGH FROM ANN
Perry Hagopian

FLIRT LIKE AN ALL-STAR
Pages 8-9: Terry Doyle
Page 10: Beth Studenberg
Page 13: Nick Onken
Page 14: Chris Eckert/Studio D
Page 15: HGP* Ernest: Chris Eckert/Studio D
Page 16: Saye
Page 17: HGP* Connor: Chris Eckert/Studio D
Page 18: HGP* Chris: Chris Eckert/Studio D
Page 19: Sarah Kehoe
Page 21: Chris Eckert/Studio D
Page 23. Nick Onken
Page 24: Beth Studenberg, HGP* Ernest: Chris Eckert/Studio D
Page 25 HGP* Connor: Chris Eckert/Studio D
Page 27: Chris Eckert/Studio D
Page 28: Nick Onken
Pages 30-31: Left to right: Keith King. Lautner: Carlos Alvarez/Getty Images, HGP* Dan: Chris Eckert/

Studio D, HGP* Guiseppe: Chris Eckert/Studio D, Keith King, Bieber: Jim Spellman/WireImage
Pages 32-33: Left to right: Lovato: Jason LaVeris/FilmMagic, Zendaya: Paul Archeleta/Getty Images, Tisdale: Jon Kopaloff/FilmMagic, Watson: Steve Granitz/FilmMagic, Fox: Jon Kopaloff/FilmMagic.
Page 35: Nick Onken
Page 36: Larry Bartholomew
Page 37: HGP* Alex: Chris Eckert/Studio D
Page 39: Nick Onken
Page 41: Nick Onken, HGP* Ryan: Chris Eckert/Studio D
Page 42: Chris Eckert/Studio D
Pages 44-45: Hudgens & Butler: Jon Kopaloff/FilmMagic, Stone & Garfield: Lester Cohen/WireImage, Eggenschwiler & Jonas: Josiah Kamau/BuzzFoto/FilmMagic.
Pages 46-47: Sarah Kehoe, HGP* Chris: Chris Eckert/Studio D
Page 48: Chris Eckert/Studio D
Page 51: Chris Eckert/Studio D

BE A SUPER-DATER
Pages 52-53: Ashley Barrett
Page 54: Cheyenne Ellis
Page 57: Beth Studenberg
Page 59: Keith King, HGP* Dan:

Chris Eckert/Studio D, Styles: Stuart Wilson/Getty Images
Pages 60-61: Beiber: Jim Spellman/WireImage, Guys: Aaron Warkov
Page 63: J. Ryan Roberts/Studio D
Page 64: Ice-cream: Douglas Johns/Getty Images
Page 65: Clockwise from top left: HGP* Joe: Chris Eckert/Studio D, HGP* Jared: Chris Eckert/Studio D, Ice Skates: David Muir/Getty Images, HGP* Ernest: Chris Eckert/Studio D, HGP* Ryan: Chris Eckert/Studio D, HGP* Guiseppe: Chris Eckert/Studio D
Page 66: Sarah Kehoe
Page 68-69: Beth Studenberg
Page 70: Nick Onken
Page 72: Ashley Barrett
Page 75: Beth Studenberg
Pages 76-77: Keith King
Page 79: Peter Rosa
Page 81: Chris Eckert/ Studio D
Page 82: Saye
Page 83: HGP* Romel: Chris Eckert/Studio D
Page 84: HGP* Mat: J. Ryan Roberts/Studio D, HGP* Kendall: J. Ryan Roberts/Studio D
Page 85: Ashley Barrett
Page 87: Saye

Page 88-89: Beth Studenberg
Page 91: Saye

HAVE THE BEST MAKEOUT
Pages 92-93: Cheyenne Ellis
Page 94: Beth Studenberg
Page 97: Chris Eckert/Studio D
Page 99: Chris Eckert/Studio D
Page 101: Sarah Kehoe
Page 103: Keith King
Pages 104-105: Beth Studenberg, Keith King, HGP* Giuseppe: Chris Eckert/Studio D
Page 106: Kevin & Danielle Jonas: John Lamparski/WireImage, Rivera & Big Sean: Gregg DeGuire/WireImage, Tisdale & French: FameFlynet
Page 109: Terry Doyle
Page 111: Chris Eckert/Studio D
Page 112: HGP* Matt: Chris Eckert/Studio D
Page 113: Chris Eckert/Studio D, Posey: Jason LaVeris/FilmMagic
Page 115: Terry Doyle
Page 117: Keith King
Pages 118-119: Sarah Kehoe, HGP* Joe: Chris Eckert/Studio D
Page 121: Beth Studenberg
Page 123: Keith King
Page 124: Larry Bartholomew
Page 125: HGP* Tyler: Chris Eckert/Studio D
Page 126: HGP* Mat: J. Ryan Roberts/Studio D, HGP* Kendall: J. Ryan Roberts/ Studio D, HGP* John, Mac: J. Ryan Roberts/Studio D, Craig: J. Ryan Roberts/ Studio D, Morgan: J. Ryan Roberts/Studio D, Hector: Chris Eckert/Studio D, Justus: Chris Eckert/Studio D
Page 127: Keith King
Page 128: Ashley Barrett
Page 130: HGP* Mac: J. Ryan Roberts/Studio D, HGP* Justus: Chris Eckert/Studio D
131: Ashley Barrett

DEFINING THE RELATIONSHIP
Pages 132-133: Keith King
Page 134: Chris Eckert/Studio D
Page 137: Chris Eckert/Studio D
Page 139: Ashley Barrett
Pages 140-141: Ashley Barrett, HGP* Jordan: Chris Eckert/Studio D
Pages 142-143: Hemsworth: Paul A. Hebert/Getty Images, Sarah Kehoe
Pages 144-145: Terry Doyle
Page 147: Sarah Kehoe
Page 149: Chris Eckert/Studio D
Page 151: Nick Onken
Page 153: Beth Studenberg
Page 155: Sarah Kehoe
Page 156: Curtis, Logan, Lane: Cheyenne Ellis
Page 157: Chris Eckert/Studio D
Page 159: Beth Studenberg
Page 161: Terry Doyle
Page 163: Larry Bartholomew
Page 165: Keith King
Page 166: J. Ryan Roberts/Studio D
Page 169: Lautner: Carlos Alvarez/Getty Images, Colette De Barros
Page 170-171: Zylka: Jason Merritt/Getty Images, Keith King
Page 172-173: Beth Studenberg
Page 175: Ashley Barrett
Pages 176-177: Beth Studenberg, HGP* Jason: Chris Eckert/Studio D

LOVE QUIZ BLOWOUT
Pages 178-179: Ashley Barrett
Page 180: Ashley Barrett
Page 183: Clockwise from top left: Tisdale & French: Allan Bregg/Splash News, Stone & Garfield: Fame/Flynet, Van Camp & Bowen: Fame/Flynet, Thorne & Klier: Fame/Flynet, McCord: Fame/Flynet, Calder & Tomlinson: Sultana/Splash News, Hudgens & Butler: SWAP Splash News, Kunis & Kutcher: © Brian Rowan/Candidwire/PacificCoastNews.com, Rivera & Big Sean: Robyn Beck/AFP/Getty Images, Hyland & Prokop, Andy Kropa/Getty Images.
Page 184: Keith King
Page 186: Keith King
Page 187: Larry Bartholomew
Page 188: J. Ryan Roberts, HGP* Ishmael: Chris Eckert/Studio D, Eliseo: Chris Eckert/Studio D, Trevor: Chris Eckert/Studio D, Jared: Chris Eckert/Studio D, HGP* Michael: Chris Eckert/Studio D

*HGP: Hot Guy Panelist

SEVENTEEN

EDITOR-IN-CHIEF ANN SHOKET

CREATIVE DIRECTOR JESSICA MUSUMECI

EXECUTIVE EDITOR BETHANY HEITMAN

BOOK DESIGN BY KELLY ROBERTS

TEXT BY DEVIN TOMB

PHOTO EDITOR ANTONELLA D'AGOSTINO

THANK-YOUS

Jessica Musumeci, Bethany Heitman, Alison Jurado,
Sally Abbey, Kelly Roberts, Devin Tomb, Antonella D'Agostino,
Carissa Rosenberg Tozzi, Marisa Carroll, Meaghan O'Connor,
Alexis Benveniste, Mark Gompertz, Jacqueline Deval,
Chris Navratil, Frances Soo Ping Chow, Cindy De La Hoz,
and the whole Running Press team.